May Peace, Love &
always be with you.

Namaste!

Peace

be still

*A path to self-awareness, love,
abundance, and harmony*

Jeremy E. McDonald

Lamplight Group
www.lamplight-group.com

Published by: Jeremy E. McDonald
www.jeremymcdonald.net

Peace Be Still
Jeremy E. McDonald
Second Edition

References used in this book include biblegateway.com, inspirational-quotes.info, and headless.org
Author photo © 2012 Julian Robles Photography. All rights reserved.
Cover design and text layout © 2012 Anne L. Louque. All rights reserved.
Cover images © 2012 istockphoto.com; bigstock.com. All rights reserved.
Edited by: Steve Hammond, Danielle Merkle & Justin Duncan, Elizebeth Vittoria Cope

ISBN-13: 978-0692706442
ISBN-10: 0692706445

Printed in the United States of America

Peace

be still

A path to self-awareness, love,
abundance, and harmony

Jeremy E. McDonald

Dedicated to my mother

Laurie Jean McDonald

She raised me to be:
"Be proud of who I am"

This made me the man I am today.

◆━━━━━━━━━━━━━━━━━━◆

June 23, 1957 – January 9, 2012

Table of Contents

> *For those who believe, no proof is necessary. For those who do not believe, no proof is possible.*
> *John and Lynn Saint Clair Thomas*

Introduction

This book comes to me after several years of experiencing life. I learned through chaos, depression, and anger finally to let go and say, "Okay God whatever you want me to do I will do." I say this because I have been a very stubborn student. As I look back, the information and signs were there for me but I did not want to see them. My own fear got in the way of seeing the basic principles that would have kept me in the flow of life so I could easily love myself and lead a joyous life.

Sound familiar? Haven't we all been hard students? Haven't we all looked back in retrospect and said, "Wow, if I only had the wisdom I have now, my life would be different." Now, I cannot speak for you, but what I do know is, I would not have been who I am today if I had not had yesterday happen. Without going through all the emotional trauma of thinking, "I was not good enough," to thinking that there was a God that hated me because of what I perceived the bible said, I would not have been able to let go enough to write this very book and experience the life of miracles I experience on a daily basis.

So how was this book inspired? In July of 2006, I looked at myself in the mirror and said to myself, "My life is not where I want it to be, and I am totally miserable." I did not really know what to do, other than the fact that I really did not like my job at all, my relationship had been suffering, and I was living with a roommate that seemed to be very hostile towards me. I had created what I called then, hell on earth.

Yes, you heard me; I created the world that was around me. Living away from my friends and family in Baltimore, Maryland, I had been chasing a dream that despite all the signs was very much out of alignment with who I truly was. In that moment, even though I did not realize it at the time, I had changed my world, because it set in motion the next four years of my life.

Shortly after that, my relationship ended and my job ended. I obtained a new job, only to lose it three weeks later. I had a good deal of my material objects stolen, lost my home and had my car repossessed. If that was not bad enough, the roommate I had, one of my closest friends, ended up not speaking to me ever again. This was what I originally called six months of hell.

There were some days I could not even get out of bed. I would literally try to pick myself up out of bed and physically fall back because I did not have enough energy to do so. I was at an all-time low. Finally, I did what any person would do who was running from the truth, I started doing drugs. I did meth amphetamines, drank a lot, and hung out with several people that liked to party and have a good time. One night I went out with some friends and got totally messed up. They had to call someone to come get me because they were worried about me driving. Because of this incident, I was reminded by my higher self that five months prior I promised God I would follow him no matter what. I also promised to teach other people how to be liberated and free in life, because that was exactly what I wanted out of life.

I had to start really looking at my life, where I was, and be truly honest with myself. I had just spent the last six months of my life in a stage of self-pity and grief, and had pointed my finger at everyone else, blamed them, but never once looked at myself. My higher self, did everything possible to get me to look

2

from the inside going out instead of looking at the outside going in. I started asking myself honest questions, "What am I so afraid of? How did I get here? Where I am to go from here?" The answers came to me through experiencing life, and not always an instant answer in my head.

What I found out later is the answer was always truly there, but I did not hear it or see it. I spent more time thinking about what was going on with my outside world, that I missed what was going on and being said in my inside world. What was happening in my inside world was my soul was screaming for me to let it out and allow it to be free. I continued to learn and continued to open up a little bit at a time, and what God brought me is an abundance of teachers and friends that showed me through the classroom of life.

I learned to hold myself accountable, and look from the inside out, and not from the outside in. At first, I wondered what that meant, because I had spent most of my life looking at things outside of myself, desiring them so much that I was missing what was right in front of me.

What was missing? Me! Every aspect of me. Every thought, every experience, and every moment of the "RIGHT NOW" was what I was missing. I desired a relationship, the expensive car, or whatever else was not coming from the inside.

When I would hear people tell me that I have to love myself before any of those things can be in my life the right way, I did not understand what they were saying. I would tell myself that I do love myself, and I would love myself even more with all of the worldly things I desired. There is a bible verse from Matthew, Chapter 7 (NIV). Jesus states that a wise man is one who builds the foundation of his house on rock.

When my teacher and friend, Virginia Drake, reminded me of this teaching, I did not totally get it at first. Then I realized my foundation was forming on rock. I had been doing the work. At that point, I knew who I was, because I found myself. Through all of the heartache, crying, anger, and fear, I was finally alive for the first time in my life.

This time it could not fall down around me again because I was standing on a firm foundation of love that I did not have before. I know now that my own love for myself, and my own divinity, are within me, and I love and accept every aspect of who I am. Now my foundation is of rock. The rocks are: truth, love, peace, harmony, synergy, joy, and awareness. These are just human words, but it is what I feel.

When I realized that this book idea I had in my head for several years finally clicked in, my head and the flow of divine information started coming to me, what to say and how to say it, and where it was to come from. I had no doubt this is what I was going to do, and lost all doubt and expectation on the outcome. I knew how I was going to complete this project.

When I realized that, and realized I had let go and gained a great love for myself, it was then this book came alive, because I had come alive.

Please enjoy, and may these teachings from my soul be of benefit to all sentient beings.

> *Now this is not the end. It is not even the beginning of the end. But it is, perhaps, the end of the beginning.*
>
> *Winston Churchill*

Chapter 1
Back to the Beginning

When I think back on my childhood and growing up, I have to really process, and think about what it was that held me back. How did the world hold my soul back and keep me from developing into what my soul already knew I was?

I think, often times we tend to look at what is broken, instead of looking at where we are and how we got to where we are today. The thing is, with all honesty, if I was to compare my childhood to others that I know, my childhood was amazing! My mother was very loving, and she did her best to make sure that I had a solid foundation to start my life.

I whole-heartedly feel my mother was a great mother in comparison to other mothers. I have worked with mothers who knew their children were being molested and did nothing. I have also had clients whose parents beat them, yelled at them, and hurt them repeatedly. My EGO self wants to judge parents that hurt their children, and put my mother on a pedestal. I think, "What a total angel and saint she was in comparison to those parents."

The reality is, while I am judging them and putting my mother on a pedestal, I am missing one very important aspect of my life. In my life I have felt I am less than everyone else, hurt by everyone else, victimized by everyone else, less attractive, never good enough and the list goes on in my victim mindset.

I have done everything to deny myself the very things I wanted so desperately in my life! This is no exaggeration! So, where do I begin in this story?

I was born in 1974 in Minneapolis, MN to a mother who was 16, and a father who was 15. My parents were children themselves. They really did not know who they were, let alone know how to raise a child. I was raised by my mother because my father and his parents moved to Arizona. I was born into a family where the common theme was, "A child should be seen and not heard." I heard this on a regular basis from a good majority of my family. The exception to this was my mother, who taught me that as long as I was polite, and waited my turn to speak, I had just as much right to speak as the adults did.

I know now that she even defended that stance to other members of the family. What is really amazing about all of this is, even though my mother encouraged me to do a lot of things in my life, and she always told me that I could do anything in my life, I did not believe it. Therefore, I did not really think I could do anything. I would hear my mother's words in my head, "You can do anything you want in your life if you put your mind to it." I would hear those words over and over again in my mind, but I would still hold myself back, and be afraid to step out of my comfort zone. How did this happen?

What my mother and I discovered later in life, when we both were getting involved in studying different spiritual paths, is both of us were very old souls. What I also realized is my mother thought very little of herself, as well.

Despite the fact that she had major accomplishments in her life, based on the world of man, she still thought very little of herself. The words that my mother taught me, she did not believe herself! Neither of us believed in ourselves, so we were constantly holding each other in a pattern of being less than. Further proof of what is going on inside you, is the real message we send out to others. This message is less about the spoken words, and more about the feelings inside the person sending the message.

As both of us have worked on our own lives, we both grew in awareness of ourselves, and we talked about these very things. We were both very co-dependent with each other. Even though we did not realize what we were doing; I was holding her back, and she was holding me back, and we were doing it all in the name of love. As we became more aware, I noticed our relationship of mother and son became richer and fuller.

So, who taught me to be small? Was it my mother? Was it the world that said everything was hard? Was it the people that told me my ideas of the world were stupid or crazy? Was it the fact I was diagnosed with dyslexia back when they didn't really understand dyslexia? Was it because I thought and felt in my mind that the world thought I was stupid? What about the teacher who put me in the corner when I was a child, because I talked too much?

Asking myself all of these questions, one day I finally woke up and realized it was none of the above. I was making myself feel small. It was at that point I really started to change my life.

Something even more amazing is the morning, when I sat down to write this chapter, my mother sent me an email with the following scripture from the Bible. In John 16:33 (NIV), Jesus said, "These things I have spoken to you that in me you may have peace. In the world, you will have tribulation but be of good cheer, I have overcome the world."

What does Jesus mean by this? He is stating exactly what I discovered in myself. He was no longer a victim of this world, and he could let go of all the expectations of this world and just experience it as an observer in love. When he did this, he realized that Love does not judge, it does not take any tallies of wrong doings, and that he could live in this state of eternal love allowing himself to experience his human existence to the fullest. As a result, he was able to let go of everything and ascend back into oneness with God. What this taught me is, as a child, I had a message to speak, but it was not yet time for me to speak it. I needed to discover my human side and bring that human side into oneness with God and my Soul. As I did this, I began to understand how to bring all of who I am into oneness, and stay in a constant flow with the whole of me.

What I learned was not to let the expectations of others hold me back. I learned to say how I felt, even if it upset people, but also to say it with compassion through the heart. As I learned how to speak up and tell my truth in love, I started to tell my body, mind, and spirit to experience joy, and my life started to change. It continues to change on a daily basis. This is far different from the world I experienced beforehand.

I watched my mother go without eating, just so I could eat. I watched my mother's heart break when she had to tell me "no" to things, even though she really wanted to say "yes." I know my mother felt bad because she could not give me what I wanted because she did not have the money she felt she should.

This is the world we have created. In order to experience happiness, we feel we have to have material things in order to experience happiness. This is vastly different from what our souls want. Our souls want to be blissfully happy, and just enjoy the material world for what it is, an experience. We have made the material world more powerful than we are.

The result is we experience what should be enhancing our joy, which makes us feel like victims! This is not why God created us. He created us to experience LOVE, JOY, HAPPINESS, PASSION, and many other things, which allow us to experience the world through God's love and God's eyes. We experience this inside of ourselves, because we are of God, and because we are of God, we are God but not in the singular sense, but we are ONE with God, not separated from God.

As I grew older, life became about how powerful I wanted to be, so I could create a world where my mother would not have to go without. I wanted to become powerful so I could force the world to understand what peace and love are all about. What I did not realize, was I was forming myself into being a tyrant who would force others to my will in order to get what I wanted and I would be doing it in the idea of Love. I created this because of the smallness inside of me. This was a direct result of the pain, which I created inside myself.

Was this a result of my environment, the co-dependency I had with my family, or the schools which taught me to be quiet and not speak up? Was it because there were no resources to teach me the skills that I needed to get in touch with myself?

That is not the way I choose to look at this; I choose to look at my childhood, and how I felt, as an incredible opportunity.

Now, as I look back at my life, and look at the things I did to run from the divinity that was in me, I realize that my victim mentality was an addiction. That addiction kept me from knowing my truest self. After I realized this, I could see all the things that made me feel small were lessons I could use. I see them now for what they were: opportunities.

The world, with its limitations, was created so we all feel small, and we all feel like a victim. We create conspiracies in our minds, we create pain in our bodies, and we create a polarity in our minds which always make us right and another wrong. All of this keeps us in a state of war inside ourselves. Every time, in my life, when someone told me to be quiet and be respectful of others, the reality was, I mirrored back the very disrespect they gave themselves.

You see, no one wants to look at who they are, and what they have created inside of themselves. We can give others a message, and speak to people with compassion, because the very compassion we give them, we are giving to ourselves. This is what Jesus taught us, to speak our truth. The truth sets us free, but we can do it with compassion and an understanding of knowing where other people are in their lives.

I struggled with this for a very long time, because my ego had grasped onto the feeling that I was never heard by anyone, so I would say things to make people hear me. Yet again, I was back to making people do things, but the person that was not

9

really listening, was me. I was not listening to my own inner divinity. I was not paying attention to the pain of ignoring myself.

I finally had to start listening and talking to myself on the inside and this developed a relationship inside of me. This changed everything, because as you think others are judging you and putting you down, you experience on the outside what is going on inside of you. You are putting yourself down and judging yourself 200 times more than anyone else is. You are experiencing that stress in your body, and keeping yourself fragmented from your truest self.

It has been a beautiful thing to get to know me, and every day I discover more about myself. What the world has become is a constant experience of experiencing me. Sometimes I have an experience of getting out of balance, and sometimes I have an experience of being in balance, but all experiences help me get in touch with myself on a much deeper level. This is what truly makes life joyful to me.

> *People often say that this
> or that person has not yet
> found himself. But the self
> is not something one finds,
> it is something one creates.*
> *Thomas Szasz*

Chapter 2
My Inside World

I am going to be talking a great deal about our inside world and referring to our inside world several times. In my understanding, there is very little difference between your Soul, Inner Divinity, inner voice, or even God. To me it is all one consciousness, not separate. We create the labels we put on things with our human minds. In reality, the word God means nothing to God, but as humans, we have given it strength. What is important to God is how we live and how we live from the inside, not what we show the world on the outside.

The inside world is going on deep within you. I found this to be the most important lesson I learned along the way, and it is a constant process. In other words, I look inside myself to find my happiness instead of looking to others to give me happiness. I look inside myself to find security, pleasure, success, and abundance instead of to an outside source to give me these things.

So how did I do this? The first thing I did was to realize I am the most important relationship I could ever have. I had to think about myself and heal myself before I could be of service to anyone else, or be happy with anyone else. I also, in turn, needed to be happy with myself and love myself before I could have a relationship with God. I know to some this will seem backwards, because we are taught to be of service and to think of others before we think of ourselves, and we are taught to make God the number one priority before ourselves.

I challenge you to make yourself number one, and by doing so, you will also make God number one. Let me explain what I am talking about in detail. In 1 Corinthians 3:16 (NIV) it says: "Don't you know that you yourselves are God's temple and that God's Spirit lives in you?" Here we are told that the spirit of God lives within us. What I have learned through meditation and developing a relationship with myself is the spark of God is within us and is very much a part of us. When we water and tend the spark within us, it will grow and manifest within us. Further in our lessons we are taught in John 14:20 (NIV) the following: "I am in my Father, and you in me, and I in you." So what does this mean? What it means is that we are all one consciousness existing in a cohesive body. Therefore, the SELF is really a part of the whole, and in reality it serves itself in Love and then it honors the whole. Lastly, we are told in 1 Corinthians 12:12-14 (NIV) that the whole body of Christ if made up of many parts but that it is still just one body. Meaning we are all One. I have researched many different spiritual faiths and the general theme is that we are all just ONE body or ONE consciousness.

As we learn to LOVE ourselves and have a relationship with our inner divinity, our world begins to change. As I learned to listen to my inner voice more than my outside stimulus, I began to change how I felt about myself on the inside. I had a film crew video record my lectures. It was then I finally realized how much I changed in my life. Previously, if I saw myself on camera, I would have looked at the video and cringed. I would have worried if my message was good enough. I would not have wanted to look at the video and definitely would have criticized my presentation. However, at this point I kept looking at the video and getting more and more excited about what I was saying on the video. I even learned a few things from my own teachings, and asked myself, "I said this?" It was an incredible feeling! I finally started seeing myself how others were seeing me. Finally, I was starting to see myself and enjoying who I am right now! This went on even deeper in my life than just my presentations. I was even looking at myself in the mirror and for the first time seeing a beautiful person and even physically good looking person. I even started noticing that the mind chatter was less than it used to be. No longer did I have the constant voice in my head telling me I am not good enough. You know the voice I'm talking about, the one that says, "I can't do this because I am not smart enough. I do not have a enough money. No one will hear what I am saying. I do not have the college education others have. I am not them, will never be them, and why get my hopes up when I know that dream will never happen." You know the one I'm talking about, because we all have that voice of limitation in us. It's that mind chatter constantly talking in our ear telling us about what we cannot have. That voice usually stems from fear.

So what changed from the past to the present? At this point, I now understand that it is my inner divinity (my soul) that is talking and not my EGO. I am no longer trying to think of content to WOW my audience and make myself look better in their eyes. Instead, I am just getting up there and talking from my heart. In other words, I am allowing my inner divinity to speak through me. In reality, I am allowing the whole of God to speak through me. I am the vessel to deliver God's message.

So is God an outside force? No! God is me and I am God. What is God to me? Well, I have affectionately started referring to God as G.O.D. (Goodness Over Doubt) because I heard a friend make this statement and it stuck with me. What God is to me is the goodness that overcomes the doubt within me. Now what really makes this incredible is that the Hindu word Guru means: One who transcends himself or herself from darkness or ignorance into light (awareness). This was incredible to me because what I realized is as I become more self-aware of myself

13

and discover more about me and what makes me work on the inside, the more I saw my world change around me.

Until a few years ago, I lived from an outer perspective. I always looked to others for acceptance, always looked to the outside stimulus to give me a false sense of happiness, pursued outer beauty instead of the inner beauty. I spent hours and hours of time wishing for a better life than I had at that moment. We filter this constant need for an outside source through several addictions which distract us from the very thing we want the most: love. People argue this very point with me, but what I discovered was every person I encountered, if they really looked at the root of all of their desires, what they are actually seeking is love. Even those who say they would rather have money than love, still do not realize that at its very basis, they are looking for something to fill a void in their lives. They think that money and material objects will be able to fill the void. They keep exactly what they think they want on a surface level, but never find what they are looking for until they realize it is Love. The important thing to realize is we want the most intense kind of love, and that love comes from within ourselves not from outside ourselves. How can we ask another to love us if in our deepest level of self we do not even love ourselves? We look in the mirror and tell ourselves we do not like who we see. We wish we were something different! Whether it is being skinnier, heavier, more hair, blonde hair, better parents, better family, smarter… the list keeps going on and on and on. So, is it society that is beating us up on the inside by the standards that are set, or is it the person standing looking at their self? The answer is you and I are responsible for our own happiness. We have to start by looking at the reasons why we abuse our self and start changing that into loving our self.

In my case, I did not feel loved other than from a few people that were close to me. I constantly sought that connection with someone. I was definitely promiscuous to the extreme, in my pursuit to find that connection with someone. I constantly felt inadequate. With each lover I had, I based my self-esteem on them and how physically attractive they were or how young and trendy they were. I never looked inside of them and saw who they were as a soul. My lovers went into the hundreds as I searched and searched for that right soul to make a connection. My behavior was so severe that I caught STDs that fortunately were treatable by antibiotics. In my case, I am very fortunate, because I did not always use protection. This behavior, I realized, was careless and definitely not self-love. The way I lived was self-destructive. So many people would disagree with me and at the time, I would have agreed with them. I would have said, "Well it is just sex! It is just a drug what is the big deal?" The big deal is, while I was going down this path I missed the fact the right one was right in front of the mirror. It was me!

Why this story is so important is, as I pursued the one thing I thought I wanted, I had created a struggle within myself. That struggle had blocked me from the very thing I wanted and desired deep down in my Soul. As I pursued lover after lover, and tried to make a connection with them, I had a careless attitude about who I was with and how I was with them. I was going against the fact that what I really wanted was a connection with another person. Ultimately, what I wanted was a connection with another Soul. It is hard for us understand that, even though we can connect to a Soul during sex, it is definitely not going to happen until you understand your own Soul. Likes attract, so when you are careless with yourself you attract and bring into your life other people that are careless in their life.

In other words, if you are constantly in struggle on the inside of you, then your outside world will always be in struggle. As I denied myself a connection with another's Soul I jumped from one person to the next. I never took the time, or allowed myself, the opportunity to make that connection. I thought sex was the source of the connection, I continued to look for someone to complete me. What really was detrimental was I measured my self-worth by how good looking my partner was. This is what Einstein referred to as the definition of insanity, because I did the same thing repeatedly, expecting different results.

Now this is the cool part! Exactly how I feel on my inside is exactly how my outside world unfolds! How I changed, my life is with this simple understanding; I just listened to myself and heard what I said to myself on the inside. This is not as hard as you may think, because all I did was pay attention to how I felt. I listened to the mind chatter going on inside of my head and all the judgment that piled up deep inside my body. You know the feeling I am talking about, all those times we say in the aftermath we could have handled something better. All those times we say to ourselves that we need to lose weight because we are not healthy enough or attractive enough. Those times we make ourselves feel guilty for not doing the things we think we should be doing and measuring ourselves to what the world expects. There is a war going on inside our minds, but we have the power to stop it!

So, as I heard the mind chatter over and over again in my mind, body and soul, I realized I spent more time telling myself what I was not, or what I should be, or could be, that I did not spend any time living in the moment! I was like "WOW!" It was a huge moment of clarity! How, if I spent all this time torn up inside and barely enjoyed the moment, and only looked to the future to what I don't have right now, and held onto the woes of yesterday, could I ever be happy? Well you know the answer. I could never be happy.

Happiness can only happen in the present moment and I will never find or accomplish any of my dreams if I constantly focused on the result and never enjoyed the experience and adventure. What we experience on the journey is what gives us the strength to achieve our goals! This is a massive blessing! I now know that inside of me there was a program repeating itself, preventing me from having the happiness I always wanted! This *was* HUGE! It **is** HUGE!

So what happens when you flip your inside thoughts from constant judgment to Unconditional Self Love? Love from deep within you will never judge you, and will never ask anything from *you* other than having a relationship with it. I can tell you, it has been one of the most incredible journeys I have ever experienced in my life. I would not trade the relationship I have with myself for any other relationship on this planet; all others pale in comparison.

Once I had changed my inside to love, and felt that love deep within me, my relationships with other people began to get better. I found new people around me that were just as loving and were practiced the same things I was did. In fact, many of my relationships changed around me. Some of my old relationships were still around me, but I found many new ones around me as well. Why is this? As I said before, exactly how I felt on the inside was exactly how my outside world would manifest. Because I loved myself more on the inside, and made that connection with my Soul/inner divinity, I found myself doing that same thing with all the other people around me. I was finally living the life I was pursuing. Honestly, I found myself so connected with my inner world that I lost the feeling of loneliness I had many years prior. There were no more nights of sitting and wishing. I was living the life I always wanted, and it had nothing to do with the car I drove or the house I lived in, or the clothes I wore, and definitely had nothing to do with the person who laid next to me in bed. I was totally okay with myself right then and being with myself at that moment.

Because of this feeling of wholeness, I experienced inside of myself, the feelings of jealousy were no longer there. The constant reactions of anger were gone. This was because the struggle inside me had been drastically been reduced in me. I have given you a lot of information. You might be asking again, how did I do this? How can anyone do this? Here is the deal, and I know this to be true: If I can do this, anyone can. If I can pick myself up and start going inside myself and asking myself why I am doing these things to myself, and asking myself the hard questions of what brought me to this point and letting things go, I know that everyone reading this book can do the same.

My inside world was starting to change. As a result, the world changed into a world of miracles.

> *There are no seven*
> *wonders of the world in the*
> *eyes of a child there are*
> *seven million.*
> *Walt Streightiff*

Chapter 3
Living in a World of Miracles

One of the coolest things I had ever experienced was to look at someone in the middle of, what I called, "Being a drama queen." What really floored me, as I looked at them and shook my head, I realized people in a panic about money and never having enough, was the same thing I used to do. I was a drama queen! So totally paralyzed in my life to spend any money, even to pay my own bills, I would hold onto money until the very last minute, then spend it on frivolous things. I further fed the idea of "Never having enough!" One day I analyzed it; I felt my body tense up on the inside as I went to swipe my debit card at a clothing store. I felt it, and it was so obvious to me that I had an anxiety inside me happen right there in that moment. I took a deep breath and allowed myself to proceed, and as I did, the anxiety sub-sided. What was even more incredible is, when I went out to lunch with my friends later, someone bought me lunch, which was very close to the amount I spent earlier on clothes. I was totally amazed to realize, what I spent earlier, I gained at lunch. In reality, I never lost it in the first place. This was the first lesson I learned; I always had enough. Then it hit me; there has never been a time in my life that I was not provided for. I always had food in my belly, a roof over my head, clothes on my back and people who loved me. My feelings of "lack" come from my ideals of the way things should be, or what I longed to happen, but was not based on my expectations. This feeling of "lack" kept me from appreciating what I had in the moment. Therefore, I spent my life in disappointment, not the life I was born to have. We are born to enjoy life and feel it to the fullest and live up to our potential!

I had studied all kinds of spiritual texts and have done rituals to bring a happier life, to bring money and abundance. I have studied the Law of Attraction, Quantum physics and have been to numerous psychics and mediums. I have found, at least for me, that all of this is way too hard. I also realized that once I had my own inner world in balance and in love, I learned a very profound phrase I am very partial to, and it's what I call being in FLOW. It is one of the easiest concepts to me and if there is one thing I like in life, it is "easy." I do not want to do it "hard" anymore. I have spent years and years in struggle, playing the game of making it hard, and it was very much like rowing a boat upstream; you keep working hard but you do not get very far. Being in the "flow" is basically the exact same as anything else I have studied, with one subtle difference . . . this rang true to my heart. What I discovered though, is I had to heal myself first before I was effectively able to create the world around me in "flow".

You have to change your thoughts and feelings about yourself before you can change your world. What happened previously with all my other studies, was that I tried to *make* things come to me. However, as we have already covered in the last chapter, our inside world directly effects our outside. To make something come to you gives the feeling and immediate impression that you do not have it! The reality is that there are miracles happening around you all the time. You are abundant in all things! It is only our human mind that tells us we do not have enough, even though we have plenty. Each individual makes a choice to live in "lack," and it starts from within. If you are going *without* on the outside it means you will have to

20

change how you feel on the inside prior to changing your outer world.

Therefore, I just started to expect miracles to happen, but had no set expectations on how they would come, or what they would be. I have so many stories that create a living testament of how true miracles can exist for each of us. Once, my friend Justin and I decided we wanted to go to as many concerts as we could. For almost 9 months, that is what we did. We had tickets handed to us, went to local coffee shops, got very inexpensive tickets, and even were guest listed at a concert. All we did was say, "It would be cool to go to many concerts because we both love music." We just let the thought manifest. Several months later, we realized not only had we been to a ton of concerts, we had done a ton of other things as well, and we met many new friends. Our whole world was opening up right in front of us, and all we had to do was start to say "yes" to ourselves and stay in "flow." The key element is we just enjoyed life. We were grateful for the opportunities that happened in front of us. This was cool stuff!

There are miracles all around us; rainbows, dolphins the ocean etc. I lived in Florida for twenty-one years and never saw a dolphin. One day I was at the beach and I saw a dolphin jump right in front of me. It kept on jumping up and going back into the water. I will always treasure that as a magical moment! I had turned into a little child again and was, and still am, in amazement of how the world has become this beautiful majestic place. This allowed me to finally say I love how God works! This is what Jesus was trying to teach us in Matthew 18:3-4 when he says, "Truly I tell you, unless you change and become like little children, you will never enter the kingdom of heaven. Therefore, whoever takes the lowly position of this child is the greatest in the kingdom of heaven." (NIV) This is because the Kingdom of heaven is within us, not outside of us. We find our heaven deep within us when we find peace with ourselves. When we find this, the miracles come alive for us as we experience life and see the world as a child would.

21

This life I am experiencing now, is a far cry from my world before. I always looked at what happened *to* me and not *for* me. In my mind I chose to be a "victim." All I did to change was change my mind set. Sure, it did not happen overnight. There are still days I fall into a struggle in my mind, but I take a step a back, realize what I am doing and move on. I do not even beat myself up about falling into what I call old "patterns." I just look at it as an opportunity to get to know myself better, and the deeper I get, the greater the miracles. I call this "practicing the self-awareness game." Most of us call it setbacks, I call it opportunities. It changes the mindset and keeps me from judging myself. These techniques help me change my internal programming, and help me change who I am as a person. It is very easy for anyone to change their internal programming. I reiterate . . . change the way you think.

How to play the self-awareness game; stop looking at everything as if it is working against you. Start looking at every challenge as an opportunity to grow. Take every stumbling block as a way to stand up, brush off the dust, and come out stronger inside. Things happen in the highest and best order for all of us! If you look at the world as "broken," then the world will always be broken *for you.* I know some of you are saying this is all just more of that positive thinking mumbo jumbo and does not work. Even some of you who get all jazzed up and excited about what I am saying, have a voice in your mind saying to yourself is this even possible? **That, right there, is your mind chatter.** This limited voice wants to hold you back and keep you in the same old pattern you have been in all your life. Some would say that this is the devil corrupting your mind and swaying you from the goodness in you. I know this to not be true, because it is most definitely you saying these things inside to yourself. One of the greatest lessons I learned was everything that went on inside of me I *caused* and *created.* No outside source made me feel bad, only *I* did. To blame it on the devil is not taking responsibility for my thoughts and feelings, or my own decisions. This is another form of addiction that keeps me from seeing the truth.

God created us in God's image, and that being said, we were given God's ability to create the world around us. I think one of the greatest scriptures in the bible is Psalms 82:6 which says, "You are 'gods;' you are all sons of the Most High." (NIV) Why do I like this so much? Because it is commanding us to recognize who we are: children of God! We are not something small, not a peasant and definitely not a soul that is anything less than perfect! It is only our own thoughts of guilt, shame, fear etc. that put us in the place of smallness, which we experience today. That being said, the word *sin* means estranged from God. In reality, if we look at the emotions, fear, guilt, shame etc., we find they are the sins that keep us from the wholeness of what we are in Oneness. We are divine royalty; so act like it! Expect to be treated as such! This comes with the responsibility to manifest the glory of God which is within each of us at such a magnificent level, we shine bright amongst the world. When we expect miracles, and just live in the constant understanding that miracles are an everyday occurrence, then everything becomes glorious to us.

You see, it is our smallness that makes us sinners, but our understanding of our greatness is what brings us back into alignment with the whole of God. It is very much like a child who thinks so lowly of himself, he keeps repeating the patterns to self-destruction. How does it make his parents feel? Even though the parents know their child has to live his own life, I am very sure it makes them feel compassion for their child. While he is struggling, it brings tears to the parents' eyes to watch their child hurt himself repeatedly. This is very much how God sees his children as they play it small, continually harming themselves, over and over again. Thinking in their mind, "Nothing can happen for me and nothing can ever change, because this is just the way it is." I finally realized that I did not have to live like this anymore and I was greater than I could ever have imagined. In that moment I just declared, "I am whole, healthy, and perfect!" That was something I heard a friend tell me. They said it on a regular basis. What happened was something amazing, I felt a very warm and energized feeling radiating from deep inside of me. I felt it all over my body! This is because instead of me saying I was not good enough anymore, or not perfect, I was declaring exactly what I am, a perfect child of God!

Think of it this way, we were created perfect by God, and saying we are anything less than that is saying God is imperfect! We are looking at our Creator and saying the design that he created was wrong! In fact, we are the only ones who say we are wrong! Only we choose to live in misery affected by what the material world thinks is perfect.

When we see perfection all around us, the world changes to miracles and perfection. As everyone in the world continues to declare war with each other and people are starving in the streets, the only one who can choose to change anything is each individual. But wait, there is more we can do. We change ourselves as individuals, and guess what else that will change? That is correct, we change the whole, and that means by changing ourselves and creating love within ourselves, we will change the world into love. We learn this in Matthew 18:19-20 "Again, truly I tell you that if two of you on earth agree about anything they ask for, it will be done for them by my Father in heaven. For where two or three gather in my name, there am I with them." (NIV). There we have it. We learn that if as few as two of us change how we feel, agree on, and get into alignment with what we ask for, it shall be done! It can't get any easier than that! Some of us are still out there fighting for a better world, and standing on picket lines, judging others, saying what others are doing is wrong. By arguing about which political party is right or wrong, we are missing the fact that if we change ourselves we can change the world. This is exactly what Gandhi meant when he said, "Be the change you want to see in the world." He is saying if we change ourselves, be *that* change, *live* that change, be witness unto the world, we will change the world!

Create a world of miracles and make it happen inside of you by declaring it right now, by saying inside your mind right now, "I expect miracles and open my eyes to see miracles in each moment." When you speak it inside yourself, you will be talking to your inner world and declaring going forward this is how you choose to live.

Chapter 4
Projection

I think one of the hardest lessons I learned, has to do with the subject of projection. It is massively difficult for the EGO to grasp onto this concept because it sees things through our own filter of what is right and wrong. The reality is there is no right or wrong in the eyes of God, only FEAR or LOVE. FEAR keeps us from our true nature, bringing us heartache, stress, strife, and feelings of inadequacy. LOVE empowers us and gets us closer to God letting us see our fullest potential. We have a choice as to what path we take, and our Souls have free will. I choose to follow my own inner voice and that voice is at one with God. This is how I choose to live. It is the voice of our soul, our higher self, or whatever we choose to call it. This voice leads us to salvation and a life filled with abundance, joy, happiness, and love.

So, what is projection? The easiest way I explain projection is with an old phrase I learned a long time ago, "As I point my finger out in judgment then I most definitely have three pointing back at me. When I am judging another, I am also judging myself." I practiced this on a daily basis, and by doing so I realized how much I judged myself and how I was truly not working in my highest and best potential in life. I had a moment that helped me realize this: One day I was at my office after teaching an all weekend retreat. I felt amazing inside and felt this good feeling from deep within me. A woman walked by wearing an outfit that a colleague of mine thought was hideous. As my colleague said it, I shook my head in agreement and continued the joke, "What was she thinking when she looked in the mirror this morning?" Immediately afterwards I told myself, I should not have said that. Right in that moment, all those good feelings I had inside of myself ended. I felt my body clench up and a heavy feeling came over me. I realized in that moment it was not God, it was me! My judgment of what I said about her came back on me tenfold and it wasn't karma, it wasn't the man in the sky judging and bringing a changed feeling on me; it was ME! We are our own critic, judge, jury, executioner, and SAVIOR!

You alone can pull yourself out of any misery you have in your life. You alone are the only one who can make yourself feel bad. Constantly I work with who people who talk about others and say the other person is making them feel miserable! In reality, it is they who make themselves feel miserable. As they point their finger in anger and get upset accusing the other of treating them badly, they are the ones who feel anger in their body and they are the ones who cause damage in their body from all the anger that they feel inside. Trust me, the stress they put on themselves hurts them more then it hurts the other person. So who is causing this? They are, because they have total control over their emotions. Their reactions bring them into this state of non-awareness. As they project out onto others and continue to blame someone else for their problems, they are continually being the constant victim.

In today's culture, we see this constantly! People upset because they feel corporations are taking away and causing the lack. People feel that politicians are corrupt! If it is not the democrats saying something about a republican then it is the republicans saying something about a democrat. The same is true with the rich and poor. The poor think the rich have everything and the rich think the poor have everything. I even had a wealthy boss who felt his employees just wanted to keep sucking money out of his pocket and draining him of everything he earned. Even though he had a lot of money in the bank, in his

27

mind he was very, very poor. This made me finally realize our wealth did not come from our material possessions, but directly from how we felt inside ourselves. This was powerful! You hear this phrase repeatedly, but until you see it with your own eyes, and realize it in your heart, it does not totally sink in.

We start changing this by really looking at ourselves in the mirror, taking the time to look at our projections on a deeper level! Remember, every single time you point your finger in judgment; you immediately have to stop and look at yourself! If you look at a person and feel they are being rude to you, ask yourself these questions: When have I been rude to someone else? When have I been rude to myself? When have I abused myself? When have I talked down to myself? If you really take a hard look at yourself, you do this constantly. When you see that person, you feel is being rude to you that as an opportunity to use them as a mirror of how you are treating yourself on the inside.

Remember how we feel on the inside is exactly how our world on the outside unfolds. If you accuse someone of cheating you, stealing from you, or lying to you, then you have to ask yourself. "When have I done these things to myself?" Now some of you might be saying to yourself, "Wait a minute! I have never stolen from myself or lied to myself, how is this possible?" A few years ago, I would have totally agreed with you, but then I realized, every time I did something I did not want to do because I was trying to keep someone around, or please another, I was cheating myself. Every time I allowed a person to treat me poorly and I did anything about it, I was cheating myself and lying to myself, by saying that I would be okay. When I started digging deep into myself, I realized that those things really hurt, but I buried them deep inside of myself. I also stole from myself because I let my life fly by without enjoying every moment. By constantly looking forward to the future, I was denying myself living in the present moment. I was stealing my own life away from myself!

The reality is, we are always projecting. You as a being, are one giant projector. Since you are projecting out to the world how you feel on the inside, the question you have to ask yourself is, "Do I want to project the fear inside of me, or do I want to project the love inside of me?" If you project the love inside of yourself, then you will also experience love all around on the outside. When we release and face our fears, our world changes to a different projection as discussed in the previous chapter.

This is a far different life from being enslaved by your fears and outside stimuli and being in constant reaction. The abuser in your life is you. You create exactly what happens all around you at all times just by your reactions and how you feel on the inside.

Now this does not mean we allow others to abuse us, because one of the ways to change how we feel on the inside is to speak our truth. What this means is, we look at our own reactions, and we practice self-awareness and before we say anything we reflect on the relationship developed inside ourselves before we talk to another. Now this could happen in a split second and it comes down to the basic principle of what Jesus taught us when he said in Matthew 7:3-5 (NIV), "Why do you look at the speck of sawdust in your brother's eye and pay no attention to the plank in your own eye? How can you say to your brother, 'Let me take the speck out of your eye,' when all the time there is a plank in your own eye? You hypocrite, first take the plank out of your own eye, and then you will see clearly to remove the speck from your brother's eye."

This teaching by Jesus is very powerful, because all he is saying is clean your house first, and then if need be, help your brother and speak your truth. Because you took the time to understand yourself better, you are able to help another. Once you understand what is going on within you, what is going on in another is easier and clearer to understand.

As we practice self-awareness in ourselves, and find compassion for ourselves, we will in turn give compassion to others. As the Dalai Lama teaches us, "If you want *others* to be happy, practice compassion. If *you* want to be happy, practice compassion." In essence, what he is saying is be compassionate. Speak your truth, and practice self-awareness with yourself, do it with compassion. Be gentle with yourself and by default, you will be gentle with others. This is very similar to what Jesus taught when he said: "Do not judge, or you too will be judged. For in the same way you judge others, you will be judged, and with the measure you use, it will be measured to you." Matthew 7:1 (NIV). Just like the story, I used at the beginning of this chapter when I judged another for what they wore; I was judged with the same measure I gave her. This brought my good feelings back to guilt and shame, and created a vicious cycle. In this case, I became aware of my thoughts, but many other times I had not and this created a cycle of unawareness that kept me from experiencing the highest levels of joy for me. What these spiritual masters taught was self-love and self-awareness. Through this, we find oneness, and with oneness, we find peace within ourselves and we become whole.

> *Opportunities are usually disguised as hard work, so most people don't recognize them.*
>
> *Ann Landers*

Chapter 5
Everything in the World Is an Opportunity

I spent most of my life in a state of thinking the world was against me, I was a victim to what someone else felt. By basing my life on someone else's opinions or what I thought their opinions were, I never really saw the possibilities. When opportunities did come up for me, I would miss them because I would be so focused on what I felt or thought was happening to me. I experienced many hours of anger brewing inside me, but on the outside, I would show everyone that I was happy and I was okay. In reality, my mind was twisting around getting upset at what was not happening for me in my life.

When I was a teenager my father said, "There are three types of people in the world, those that made things happen, those that sat and waited for things to happen, and others that sat around and said what happened?" He asked me point blank, "What type of person would you like to be?" Honestly, at the time I thought he was crazy because I was fourteen years old, and who listens to their father at fourteen? In reality, I was not listening to myself, and had no idea even how to answer my father. Instead, I got upset with him and just did not listen. He was trying to help and give me the wisdom he learned in his life. I was confused and projecting my own insecurity onto him, because I did not understand myself. Looking back on it now, I see it was an opportunity. I had a choice to either listen to him or not listen to him. I actually heard what he said but did not have the tools emotionally at that time to apply it to my life. His job was to simply plant the seed and let it grow until finally when I was in my early thirties his voice rang in my head over and over again with the very lesson he had taught me so many years ago. Some people would say it was foolish of me not to apply those lessons at the time when I heard this wisdom. The funny part is, when I look back, I was trying to apply it all the time, but saw the world as something I had to force instead of something that I had to work within. Almost twenty years later, it hit me, I did not have to force things to happen and bend to my will. I just had to get up, act on what I was seeing and experiencing, and it would come alive for me without forcing it. The very wisdom my father gave me sent me on a path of self-discovery. This was all an opportunity for me to experience life for what developed based on my decisions.

My lesson was, everything is an opportunity, and it is time to stop judging myself with, "I should have done this or if I had done it this way, things may have been better." I looked at the world differently and realized that all things are my opportunity to get to know me better and have a deeper relationship with myself.

This was big for me, and I encourage the reader to really think about this. We constantly avoid taking that leap of faith because we are scared we may make the wrong decision or the path we take will be too hard. This puts us all in a holding pattern, which keeps us from experiencing life. The point I am making is that none of your decisions are wrong, they just have a higher purpose. Even my days when I did drugs and did not honor myself were perfect. The Buddha states it well, "When you realize how perfect everything is, you will tilt your head back and laugh at the sky." I actually did this. One day I realized how everything was in divine timing and divine order and there was a divine purpose for everything. I just sat and laughed.

I spent all of these years trying to force everything and manipulate circumstances. I hid my true thoughts from people because I was judging things, not realizing how perfect they were in the first place. That in itself just made me smile and laugh a bit. The humor in knowing that I made life so much more difficult than it needed to be was very amusing. It was not a sense of judgment or wishing I would have done it differently, it was a huge wake up moment, realizing everything that happened has brought me to this point. Going forward, I choose to make life easy. Since then, I got myself caught in to scenarios and if they continued, they would bring me to a hard situation and make my life hard again. Instead, I just looked at it as an opportunity to speak my truth in love and move on. What we do in this body is practice, experiment, and see which path works best for us and keeps us in balance. This helps us grow and expand our consciousness, and helps us align with the whole of who we are.

My friend, Gina LaMonte, once said to me that in all of her studies, she has never once discovered a God that is stagnant. Every single one, in every culture, was growing and expanding. Therefore, if you are a part of the whole of consciousness, then you are expanding and growing through the experience of your life. You grow from getting out of balance, experiencing depression, sorrow and hurt. You grow from being in balance, experiencing happiness, joy and love. Most of you are trying to keep yourselves from being out of balance, but sometimes the greatest of rewards come from those moments of being out of balance. Those times you may have to go apologize to someone, you may discover an area of unawareness in yourself. The point is, that if you are trying to keep yourself from never making a mistake, then you are not living. All things you do are an opportunity to expand and grow your awareness. Our mission is to listen to our inner voice as much as possible, and allow your soul to experience it. What I did is ask my soul to guide me in the "highest and best good" for me in my divine plan, in divine timing, and in divine order. This way I do not have to worry about the details. I just experience and live life.

People have told me this is not taking life seriously. My response is always the same, "I am here to experience life and live it to the fullest. My only condition for myself is I want a deeper relationship with myself and a better understanding of God." As I enjoy life and follow my inner voice, I get to do just that, have fun and enjoy God for what God really is, a manifestation of consciousness creating a flow within the universe. If I ride the wave so to speak, we get to understand the awesomeness of what God truly is. One thing I know, God is not going to make me live in misery. Misery starts with me, not God. I have the choice to live in flow or resistance. I have the choice to make life hard or easy. If I do not live in FEAR and do not experience life to my fullest potential then I will live it in LOVE and experience the greatness of what life is all about.

If you change your focus on how you view the world, this will create a paradigm shift from seeing the world as being against you to seeing the world as an opportunity. This brings the miracles and allows you to see the world through the eyes of your soul. I realized this one day when I experienced something at my job and the person I spoke with on the phone was very rude. Normally my EGO would have jumped up into full tilt and would have wanted to have a pissing contest as to who had a bigger EGO. When the conversation concluded I would have justified my stance to myself thinking what a horrible person that was on the phone. Instead, I realized that he was being rude and this was an excellent opportunity for me to model who I had learned to be. I was able to practice my newfound peace inside and utilize what I taught other people, as a result he calmed down. The conversation went in a totally different direction than what normally would have happened. What I learned was, if I had fought with him, and had a battle of EGO's with him, it would have come directly from *my* EGO, which is "Edging God Out." The anger and the need to be better than another soul kept me from experiencing God, which is pure Love and Truth.

Within Love and Truth, there is no one is better than another, because we are all ONE. In this moment of being calm and balanced with the client, I was able to prove to myself how confident I was inside. What most people do not realize is that the confident one is usually the one that says the least and has very little to prove because they know who they are. I then evaluated the times I had experienced a battle of the EGO with someone else. I analyzed each instance. What I found each time was two people who needed to justify their stance. They needed to prove that the other was wrong so they could feel their way was correct. People who argue about religion demonstrate the fact that they are not confident in their own faith. People who have to list their credentials, show me they are not confident in their own theories or arguments. If they were confident, then they would just speak their truth and let it go, or not say anything at all.

This was a huge opportunity for me to discover something about myself on a deeper level but also allowed me to gain wisdom on how to interact with other people. This was an invaluable lesson for me. If I did not practice self-awareness, I never would have discovered this.

> *We are not human beings having a spiritual experience. We are spiritual beings having a human experience.*
> *Teilhard de Chardin*

Chapter 6
I Am a Spiritual Being Having a Human Experience

The discovery that we are spiritual beings having a human experience was profound to me. I remember sitting in meditation; totally submerged into what I call the "ONE Consciousness." I felt a collective voice speaking to me and a great feeling of love saturated my body. With every question I asked, the answers came to me with ease and with the greatest sense of compassion. I felt whole in that moment. I finally realized what the word "Holy" meant. Not on an intellectual level because I read it or someone told me but because I felt it throughout my whole being. When I awoke from this journey, I felt the bliss for many days afterwards. I felt no pain in my body and I had this great feeling of contentment. All the times before I had been wrapped up in the world around me and this great feeling had subsided. Unlike other times, this time; I realized one great piece of wisdom as I experienced this heightened state of awareness. I was bringing back infinite divine wisdom. I was coming back and it was important for me to live this new wisdom in the physical realm. It was not enough to simply understand this wisdom. I realized that I must use it and apply it and watch the seeds of my experience grow into fruit. This made the human experience that much more exciting to me because now I existed in a constant playground of experiences and constant growth.

During these experiences, I realized that my true "free will" came from living at my highest and best level of truth and with Love. I had gained a higher and deeper relationship with myself beyond anything I could ever have fathomed. You too, can have this relationship within yourself. It requires you finally say "*YES*" to yourself and take the time to understand what is the *whole* of you.

What happens with most of us, is that we see ourselves as just a small meek humans who are sinners and in the eyes of God we will always miss the mark. It is because of this that we do not see that our mistakes are also our blessings. We do whatever it takes to hide our mistakes and the result of that is that we end up building up the guilt inside of ourselves. Eventually, these kinds of feelings can begin to form a mind of their own, which will in turn box us into a penitentiary within our mind. This is what I refer to as self-imprisonment. This form of self-imprisonment continues to fester within causing very physical issues and most importantly, it creates a feeling of being trapped. This feeling will manifest around us on the outside and cause the majority to create a world of limitation and lack. That is why people tend to feel as though they never have enough and will continue to look for the way out, to finally find happiness. In turn, they continue to look at others and blame others for their situation. They blame corporations, the government, family, spouses, parents and anyone else for where they are in life, never realizing that they can change these feelings with a simple thought. When it finally hits them they gain the power to choose the way they live their lives and they begin to develop an understanding of how empowered they truly are. Their lives begin to switch to path of abundance.

I am bold enough to say this "I know without a shadow of a doubt that how we see the world and experience it, is defined by our attitude 100% of the time." If we are living life knowing it is an experience of the soul, then we *will* it to be. We will slowly stop judging how we experience it and begin to see it as a blessing or an opportunity as we have covered in the previous chapter.

In our present world right now; we weigh ourselves down by ideas of how things should be. These ideas of limitation make us hide who we truly are as people, and as a soul because we do not want people to see our true self for fear of judgment and rejection by others. We hide the things we think society will not accept for fear of what might be said ,though of or done to us as a result. We do not want to face the hurt that could come from judgment/rejection but that hurt comes from within us, it does not come from those around us. When we allow other people's feelings and opinions of us to interfere with our own happiness; we are giving those people power over us. In that moment we enslave ourselves and make the other person our master.

In my life I primarily have intimate relationships with males but I've had intimate relationships with females as well. What I found was that I had a genuine interest in males and females and could develop loving relationships with both. My church judged me for how I felt. For many years I hid the fact that I was attracted to males for fear of being judged. After I came out and was truthful about how I felt, I buried the fact that I was also at times; attracted to females. I buried that fact for fear of non-acceptance in my new community. I buried one truth to bring another forward. I was searching for acceptance but never gave myself acceptance of who I was. The truth is that I am a spiritual being having a human experience. I realized what I really love is souls that align with who I am as a soul, not their gender. Based on the world of man I would be given the limited title of being a gay male or being a bisexual male. Based on people's perceptions or based on their experiences, it would define the label they give me. I choose to be a spiritual being having a human experience. At times I choose to have experiences with souls and I do not base them on the limitations of man.

The reality is that my soul has free will. I do not need to gain the acceptance of anyone to live my life the way I see fit. I do not need a government to tell me whom I should be with, I do not need anyone else's permission for my soul to choose who I am or who I am with. I have *free will*. My choices are based on my inner voice that guides me. Even though this upsets many people, I still see myself as equal to all and I know that everyone is equal to me. We are all ONE. How we choose to live this experience is *our* own choice and no one else's. My truth does not have to be their truth. This is my experience of the soul; not theirs.

This choice belongs to all of us. You, sitting there reading this book have a choice right now to be true to yourself and live life as you see fit. What I chose for myself was to live a life in unison with my soul and to listen to my own inner voice. If I were to always follow someone else's viewpoint I would not be honoring my soul and my relationship to the divine. In these moments when I honor who I am and make choices based on what is in balance with my soul; I am giving my soul what it needs which is a trusting, loving relationship.

Some say this way of living is irresponsible or that this way of living is not possible. I am here to tell you truthfully that I am living this way and it is very much possible. Some of the desires of my EGO had to be let go in order to experience ME as a complete whole. This in itself is different than saying "I place my faith in God because God is a whole of all consciousness" We are really putting our faith into ourselves, not as an individual, but as a whole. Wholly based on what I learned, a person lives within alignment with the whole of who they are. Living in this state of being allows you to live with compassion for yourself and others and gives you a sense of clarity to proceed without judgment.

Do you see the vast difference here? When you live in FEAR, you are always going to live with limitation. When you live in LOVE, you will live a life of balance and abundance. The excitement comes from knowing you are that LOVE and by understanding and living that; you get to experience everything and not miss a thing! It doesn't matter what it is. If it is in alignment with the whole of you, then that is living a Holy life.

In our current world if someone does not agree with your path, they will very strongly state their opinion to you and in some cases try to force that opinion upon you. I've people gossip about me and say that my way as not the right way. They've also said it directly to my face. What I learned is that this is my way and if I feel in alignment with what I am doing I am not going to put out my light for anyone else. Jesus teaches us in Matthew 5:14-16 (NIV), "You are the light of the world. A town built on a hill cannot be hidden. Neither do people light a lamp and put it under a bowl. Instead, they put it on its stand, and it gives light to everyone in the house. In the same way, let your light shine before others, that they may see your good deeds and glorify your Father in heaven."

It is very important to understand when we diminish our light we do not glorify the greatness of who we are as children of God. The more in alignment, we are with God, the brighter our light shines onto the world. Let them all see the glory that is within you and empower others to do the same. Allow yourselves to live life to the fullest and enjoy every moment for what it is; a tremendous blessing!

Chapter 7
Speaking and Living Truth

Since I spent a great deal of my spiritual life studying and practicing Metaphysics, I consider myself fairly open minded. What I found truly amazing as I grew and dug deeper into myself, was the way I saw the world differently from how other people around me saw it.

During my journey, what really got me excited was that I found all of my greatest treasures and greatest wisdom within *me*. It was not in books by other people or what others taught me. I found it directly within me! Nearly all the truth I found was deep within me. As I dug deeper into myself I found more and more truth. This is how I learned about the flow of God. This is where; while in meditation, I felt that essence flow deep within and outside of me. What was really exciting was that the flow came from within me and not outside of me. When I explained this to others they either acted uninterested or totally rejected the idea! However even though I felt they did not listen, I kept telling people what I felt and saw. It was important to me that I said what I felt otherwise I felt trapped inside myself if I did not speak how I felt.

As I was speaking my truth to people, their rejection or lack of interest hurt my feelings. I had spent most of my years trying to understand other people's views and respecting where they were in their lives so it infuriated me that I was not getting the same courtesy. Why were people telling me that my ideas were stupid, wrong or just plain silly? Why were these so-called "enlightened" people criticizing who I was? It seemed very one sided to me and many times I would react in anger towards those people. I would get upset that I was not getting the same respect I had given them!

I finally realized one day that by getting angry or hurt and reacting that I myself was not strong in my own beliefs. It was about that time that I ran across this scripture in the bible: 1 Corinthians 15:58 (NIV) "Therefore, my dear brothers, stand firm. Let nothing move you. Always give yourselves fully to the work of the Lord because you know that your labor in the Lord is not in vain." To me the word "Lord" means *one who has mastered this world or one who has been Christed by allowing all of consciousness to flow through us and work through us.* Being Christed is not much different than becoming a living Buddha. So really, when we give ourselves to the work of the lord it means we allow consciousness to work through us and work within the flow of consciousness. This is the very reason why I listen to my inner voice. It knows the flow of how things work within the whole. I looked deep into this and realized it was not others questioning my beliefs, it was myself. It hit me that I allowed their issues to bring me down. At times, I did not say anything because I just did not want to argue or have my ideas shot down. Even though I heard my inner voice telling me to say something, I went against what it was saying, and therefore blocked what came through me. I did not live my truth, or even speak my truth.

What is incredible in all of this is that the Chinese teach that life force energy is "Qi." The healing art of Medical Qigong, teaches us that the flow of energy is sometimes blocked because of stagnant "Qi" within the body. "Qi" is not only life force energy, but also the energy that moves the universe. "Qi" is not much different from Consciousness or God because God is made up of pure energy and is the force behind the universe, which gives the Universe life.

This is important because when I held back my truth and held back the flow I was in essence creating stagnant "Qi" within my body. This made the very energy that gave me life; stagnant! How could I possibly have a healthy life full of enrichment and possibilities if I did not have this happen right at square one inside me? Well, the answer is: I could not have had a healthy life of enrichment and possibilities unless I had things in flow within me. It could not possibly be in flow outside of me. If I were to hold back; how many other things would I block in my life. How many other opportunities did I pass up out of the FEAR of rejection/judgement? It really makes you start think about all the areas you miss! This is where the hard questions come in. I asked myself "how can I live to my fullest potential?" Since life itself is about experiencing, where did I miss the opportunity just to LIVE?

This makes us really question just when *have* we missed opportunities when we are blocking life force energy "GOD" from working through us. We are blocking LIFE ITSELF! Why would we not want to live and experience every moment for what it is? The only answer is FEAR. Fear is the essence of what blocks us from life and what blocks us from God. God is pure love so we are blocking ourselves from Love. What we want is LOVE! So, let go and LET GOD!

How do we do this? Learning about projection is what helped me realize I had a war going on inside myself. With this understanding. I learned that those who are insecure always have to fight for what they believe in but the confident just know who they are. The confident ones do not have the need to fight with anyone or prove anything. They are just in the moment with being the happiness they have achieved. So the question I had to asked myself was in what aspect was I insecure? How did this happen? As I explained in the beginning of the book, I had great parents! More and more I realized that, yes, society teaches a system of smallness and instills it in people like myself but the real truth is that we all feel small so we only teach what we as a society or planet understand!

43

Because of this smallness inside of us, we continue to think others work against us. We think our jobs are taken from us. Government is not doing what it is supposed to do and the list goes on. The truth is we feel such a great sense of lack within ourselves and such a great sense of insignificance that we lash out at others instead of looking in the mirror at ourselves and realizing that we are profoundly amazing beings, just the way we are. In God's eyes, we are the perfection that God created and nothing less! God even tells us this in Psalms 139:14 (NIV) "I praise you because I am fearfully and wonderfully made; your works are wonderful, I know that full well."

"Fearfully" in the original Hebrew meant with great reverence and heart-felt interest. "Wonderfully" means with uniqueness and set apart as a great masterpiece! It cannot get any more plain than this! God, through the person who wrote this Psalm, was coming right out and saying you are perfect just the way you are! So, speak your truth, and live your truth, in the glory of who you are as a masterpiece created by the God most High!

Now some would say there is no God or that God has forgotten us because of what is going on in the world. The cold hard fact is this- because we create the world around us, we are the souls who allow all of this to happen on a metaphysical level. The only way to change the world is to get into the flow of God (consciousness).

Someone actually yelled at me once "You prove to me that there is something beyond and that there is a God!"

I said back to them "I do not need to prove it to anyone; I only have to prove it to myself." My job is only to speak my truth just as Jesus taught to plant the seeds and then I need to move on.

I speak what I know, after which I let the other person (soul) take responsibility for their part in the flow of energy. Whether they decide to receive the message or not is their decision. It is not for me to push them. I spent too many hours trying to convince people of the message I was trying to convey. I would get upset because they would not listen. This is exactly what Jesus taught when He said "Do not give dogs what is sacred; do not throw your pearls to pigs. If you do, they may trample them under their feet, and turn and tear you to pieces." Matthew 7:6 (NIV). "Pearls" are the wisdom we have gained from living and experiencing life! As we throw our pearls to pigs (swine) we are throwing it to deaf ears! These people are unawake to the truth you understand! You are wasting your breath trying to sell someone on something they do not want to hear or believe! All we can do is state what we know and move on! The next part of the equation is that we live our truth to the fullest and to best of our ability! The last part is that we dig deeper into ourselves and we slowly start programming with our heart "We are not SMALL! We are great beautiful beings!"

That is what this book is all about. Living life in the truth we understand to the best of our ability! We grow through our experiences and our experiences bring us to a greater self-awareness as we practice looking deep within ourselves!

When others do not share your view, let them go! We have already talked about, how arguing with them only shows the smallness in your belief system. Their path does not have to be your path! All paths lead back to God so for us to push someone does not respect the natural order of things. This will take you out of the flow. The reason: you are so focused on what they are doing that you are not spending time focusing on what you need to do!

Chapter 8
We React, Based On Our Paradigm of the World

What is mind-blowing to me is the fact that words can be so twisted! In corporate America, I taught people based on the old study that words were only seven percent of the communication process between all of us. Nonetheless, it still puzzles me how much we twist around words. This is because we live in our own paradigm. What is a paradigm? In short, a paradigm is how we see the world based on our experiences and environment. A good majority of our paradigms are created by what happened to us and how we received what happened. Every experience we've ever had in our lives has developed a part of our paradigm and in essence has created programming within us. Based on our experiences and our anticipation of the future, we create how we live in the present.

The massive problem which happens, is that we become caught-up in our paradigms. We get enslaved by the dogma which comes from the idea that our paradigm is the one truth and the only truth! Therefore, what happens is one person will say something, intending to mean one thing but the receiver of the message will totally interpret that message the wrong way. The real problem is the fact most people do not speak up about their feelings or how they understood the message they received so they never have a sense of clarity gained from that message. If they interpreted the message differently than how it was meant and they were offended by it, then they would have that inside themselves and allow it to fester. The sad part is that the person who sent the message may have no idea that it is bothering their friend. We are two people now living without clear lines of communication. This type of stuff goes on all the time. The greatest gift we can give ourselves is just share how we feel and speak up!

Recently, I had a huge moment of clarity when I posted this phrase on my Facebook, "Anything that bothers you is your issue." I got this from a book titled *The 55 Concepts* by Michael Cavallaro. A few minutes after posting this, a friend replied in comments with the following "This statement is not entirely accurate. In a relationship, if two people are unwilling to work with one another or only one person is willing to put in the effort in a relationship, then it becomes both of their problems."

I remember just sitting for a minute processing what my friend said. It was not in anger or shock and there was no reaction or judgment inside of me. I was more surprised at what was going on inside of me. I heard in my mind, "My friend is in his story as we all are in some form of our story." Then it hit me! We interpret words based on our perception of the words.

As I stated before, we get this by our experiences or non-experiences of the words. In our culture, we turn words into slang and change our languages around almost constantly. Just look at the English language today in comparison to two hundred years ago and from state to state words have different meanings and different ways they are said. It is all based on environment and culture! Instead of reacting or judging my friend, I explained my understanding of what he said "If I was in a relationship and my partner did something to hurt me I would immediately analyze why it hurt me. I define *my* happiness, not another person's. By allowing them to hurt me and not saying

47

anything I am allowing the hurt to happen inside of me. More than likely they are walking away without even realizing what they have said or done, or have moved on from what was said or done. Once I understood my own reaction I would probably still say something to my partner but for me, not them, in order to get my truth out. By understanding myself first I take the time not only to have a greater understanding of myself but also to have a richer relationship with myself." Once I explained this, my friend said he understood what I was saying now and we moved on from this conversation.

Knowing that people live life based on their paradigm or personal reality had me pondering. I realized and remembered all the times I reacted in a way that kept me from seeing someone else's point of view. I programmed myself based on the stimuli around me. If someone hurt me before and a similar experience came up again in my life, I would have a similar reaction like the response before. I might even react for fear of getting hurt again. The same might happen based on things I enjoyed or pleasurable things and I might constantly look for that pleasure again when I did not get what I was looking for. I might fall into a depression from not getting something based on my expectations.

These things happen repeatedly in our lives but we have no idea it is happening because we are living within our individual paradigm; the parts of our lives which we are not awake in. We are self-aware when we are awake. We can utilize the times we are not awake as an area of opportunity! Remember the word enlightenment means the end of pain and suffering. The "Light" part is where we shine our light and see clearly, therefore are awake. So in areas we are not awake we are not able to see clearly. Therefore; we are not only living in our paradigm, we are stuck in our paradigm.

This is what the vast majority of people are doing in life, not living in an awakened state. They are living in an ocean of their reactions happening deep inside themselves and not understanding truly what is going on within themselves. Some do not even know things are hurting them until one day something triggers the built-up anxiety going on within their bodies. Once this happens, years and years of not speaking our truth or living our truth swell up and burst out onto the world.

This is largely because most of us try to hide what we do not like about ourselves. We do not talk about the things we have done which people may look at and judge us for. This area of our lives is what Carl Jung referred to as our *shadow*. In this area of our lives, we are not able to see these things because they are hidden deep within an area we do not want anyone to see, including allowing ourselves to see. A good story to explain our shadow is the Sumerian myth of Inanna, Queen of the Heavens.

Her descent into the underworld explains to us she had to cross through seven gates to enter into the underworld to see her older sister Ereshkigal, the Queen of the underworld. When she arrived at each gate, she had to remove a piece of her royal garments such as her crown or royal robe. Eventually she reached the throne room of her enraged sister and is killed by her sister's subjects. She is stripped of all her material possessions. She eventually is saved from her situation and rises up from the underworld with a greater understanding of herself. She realizes that her sister Ereshkigal is the dark side of herself (shadow side of herself). She constantly rejected and suppressed within herself while she was trying to show the world the goodness that she wanted to project onto the world. This caused her to suppress a great piece of herself and in turn made herself stagnant inside of herself.

The result was a part of her that was so enraged when facing the neglect and stress that she had buried deep within herself that it killed her. What is important to take note of is that she shed her worldly possessions which gave her the entitlement of her royal status. The pureness of how she approached her descent allowed her to rise up out of her shadow greatly aware of what she did to herself. She was able to come back into oneness with all of herself and discover deeper parts of herself she had not been previously aware of.

49

The shadow buries thoughts deep within us and continues the programs we keep imprisoned in our paradigm. We have this idea of impressing the world and keeping an image of what we want others to see instead of our truth and being true to ourselves. In reality, your body knows when you are not being true to you and as a result you are hurting yourself and causing unnecessary stress deep within your body.

In Innana's story, the existence of the Goddess Innana is not as important as the lesson this myth brings us. I talked about this story because it relates very closely to many of our lives. We have to ask ourselves many questions in order to really discover the extent of just how much we are truly avoiding our shadow. Ask yourself, "Have I ever been upset with someone but never said anything because I was afraid of the consequences or being judged? Have I ever hid how I felt about a situation or subject because I was afraid of rejection?" Guess who rejected my opinion first? You guessed it right! It was me! Before I ever got the words out of my mouth; I had judged it and did not think it to be valid enough to say out loud therefore, rejecting and judging myself! If I were truly confident in who I was and did say something, I would know with all the confidence in the world that my views were just as valid as anyone else's. I would also be open to other views and seeing other perspectives.

This is how we grow, by opening our minds to someone else's wisdom and sharing ours. When we hide our feelings or our views, we are preventing this growth potential from happening between souls.

In some cases, it is appropriate not to say anything because you know people have to learn their own lessons. We are talking about disagreements or problems, and also talking about general conversations. I spent a great deal of years not participating in regular conversations because I was afraid I would look stupid to others. Well, guess who thought I was stupid? Me!

The real vicious cycle, is my shyness or fears, which kept people from getting to know me as a person. Even though I had friends, I still felt very lonely and misunderstood because I did not understand myself. Once I realized my voice mattered and it mattered to *me*, all my feelings of loneliness subsided. Not only did I feel smart but very smart because I was no longer ignoring my voice and myself.

I overcame most of my fears by making myself speak, even when I was unsure. Yes, as I have explained in previous chapters, I had a great deal of resistance to what I said at times. At times, friends would get very mad because instead of always being in alignment with them or in agreement with them, I would state *my* views. There were a great number of people upset. Some friendships ended because they felt I judged what they believed.

The reality is that I was changing and my friends and I were growing apart. It taught me that sometimes people (souls) come into our lives for a short amount of time. Sometimes people come back into our lives. Throughout our lives, people come and go in divine timing and divine order. Our resistance to people leaving comes from the fear of being alone or not being accepted or being branded as outcasts by society. The important part we are missing is that having a solid relationship with our Soul changes everything. This very relationship starts to recreate our paradigm from being a reactive victim mind to a wholeness-loving mind.

Why does this happen? I have explained previously that your body is a part of all consciousness, but *it* also has a consciousness. Your body is one big bag of thoughts and emotions! It is thinking and reacting to stimuli at all times! Our goal is to continue developing a deep relationship with our body and to stop denying the truth. Get back into balance with your body. In order to get back into wholeness you have to face yourself. Just like Innana, you have to go deep into your shadow. This is where you will find the programs that are going on deep within you which are making you react to the stimuli around you.

51

When you feel you are not being listened to, look in the mirror and ask yourself "Where am I not listening to myself? Where am I not paying attention to what my body, mind or spirit are trying to tell me?" This gives you the opportunity to allow your thoughts to flow and start to hear what your soul is trying to communicate with you. The most important part is creating a trust and love within yourself and by doing so, your body mind and spirit begin to work in unity. This creates a flow within your body and brings the stagnant "Qi" back into flow within the body.

Chapter 9
Mind Poison

The things we cover in this book have to do with what is going on inside of us. It is what I refer to as "mind poison" which are the thoughts we use to make excuses for ourselves. It is these thoughts which make us question our faith and get us wrapped up in what is logical or easy to see with our human eyes. The only drawback is that it keeps us from experiencing the beautiful life that God gave us. In my practice to find myself and help others; I watch people in a pattern of self-sabotage. Everyone has been in that place where things are going well and opportunities are presented but we look at those opportunities with a sense of hopelessness. This comes from our EGO and remember EGO stands for Edging God Out. What I have found is that in God, we can never go wrong! Honestly, it does not matter what spiritual faith you are. Every faith I have studied states one very important understanding—that is to give your life over to something greater than you and let it go! The hard part for your EGO is when it feels a lack of control! One thing which helped me heal was when I read Matthew 18:1-5 (NIV) when Jesus teaches us that a child is the greatest in the Kingdom of Heaven. I remember sitting there for a minute when I read this and realized a child loves and trusts genuinely and is not tainted by the cynicism that we as adults gain throughout our lives. Jesus says "He who humbles himself and becomes like a child will inherit the Kingdom of Heaven." He is saying the person that lets go of the Ego's limitations will inherit the Kingdom of Heaven. Now let us think about this for a moment. Think about a child playing and enjoying the moment of whatever he is doing. He is not thinking about bills, how to get ahead in life, how to one up someone else, or what he needs to hide so he can present a good face to the world to be accepted. No, in his purest state he is purely enjoying the moment! Society teaches us we need stuff to make us whole! As we change our inside into being more childlike and being in the moment like a child, then we can experience the world much different than we do now! This is illustrated very nicely in the Gnostic Gospels of Thomas. Jesus explains to his disciples "When you make the two one, and when you make the inside like the outside and the outside like the inside and the above like the below and when you make the male and the female one and the same so that the male not be male nor the female, female and when you fashion eyes in the place of an eye and a hand in place of a hand, a foot in place of a foot and a likeness in place of a likeness; then you will enter the Kingdom."

I know some people look at this and think, "What the heck?" Just take a second to think about it and process it. This phrase is about self-awareness and getting deeper into you. It is the realization that you are not the limitations of the labels you give yourself but you are a vast being full of unlimited potential. A child sees life as unlimited possibilities! He is not bogged down by the weight of labels, gender, race, sexual orientation or any of that. He just sees people for what they are. What I have noticed in my life is that I have dropped a lot of those hang-ups and now see people as just SOULS!

I did not always see my life this way. I remember a time when I could barely speak to someone or look someone in the eye because I saw them as greater than myself. One of the biggest epiphanies was when a family friend who is a Medical

Doctor advised me to refer to her by just her first name after I called her by her formal title of "Doctor." I thought about it for a moment and then talked to my mother who was a nurse, and realized it was because we were in a party setting with friends and family that she made the request. What occurred to me is that I had a great deal of respect for her and saw her as a great person! I looked back on all the times I looked at someone like he, and saw their degrees and thought of myself as a person who did not have those degrees. I thought to myself "I will need a degree or equivalent to get where I want to get in life." Now don't get me wrong, people who get a degree have a path just as I do and there is nothing wrong with achieving that education. This made me realize that I spent my life thinking I did not have all the elements I needed to be successful in life. What I finally realized is success was how I felt inside! It has very little to do with my status in life. What this led me to realize is how I get my life in balance on the inside and the level of how I calm the struggle on the inside is how I define my success.

Our level of accomplishment and satisfaction does not come from measurements, it comes from a clear understanding of yourself and the magnificence of who you are as spiritual being, not what you see yourself as in the physical world. In the physical/human world you measure yourself against others, defining your success based on what you see as success with your EGO or what society sets as success for you. Based on the world of man's viewpoint of the world, there will always be somebody who will be more successful than yourself. Just think about companies, credit scores, academic grades, movie stars, beauty, and everything you use to measure yourself. In the world of God, there is no status, or better or worse! In the eyes of God, we are all ONE! We are all loved by our creator equally!

So how do we change the mindset you ask? How do we begin to change our thought process and begin to live in flow with everything around us? Romans 12:2 (NIV) addresses this when it states "Do not conform to the pattern of this world, but be transformed by the renewing of your mind. Then you will be able to test and approve what God's will is—his good, pleasing and perfect will." What we learn is to renew our mind, and come into alignment with God (Goodness Over Doubt). Consciousness: We are a part of God and God is within us. Why in the world would we ever think God is against us? This would be self-defeating on God's part. The reality is, God teaches us in 1 Corinthian's 13:4-7 about LOVE. God is the essence of Love! We are taught love has no doubt, no accounting of wrongdoing, and does not delight in evil; it rejoices over the truth! What our higher consciousness wants us to realize is the hell we have put ourselves through and wants us to come back into oneness.

When we renew our mind we also renew our body and spirit. We allow ourselves to come back into balance with our highest good. What causes the flow of mind poison inside us is our need to elevate ourselves and gain a higher status in life. We constantly look outside ourselves for happiness! True happiness can never be found outside ourselves, only within! That happiness within, manifests around us and brings us the enriching relationships we so desire. When we find this level of happiness, our relationships are stronger because we are stronger inside!

We learn in Philippians 2:5: that When we are in our relationships we should treat them as Christ Jesus would have treated them. What do we learn here? Let us take a moment to think about this as well. If we created love within ourselves and transmuted our inside world from FEAR into LOVE as Jesus did, we would treat others as we felt about ourselves on the inside. As we are practicing what we learn about loving ourselves, we give that same experience to others who witness love. The only things that prevent us from doing this are forgetting who we are and being tied up in our minds with man's world and man's rules! There is nothing wrong with the physical world. These lessons teach us: Do not let any influence of this world diminish who you are on the inside as a child of God!

The renewing of our mind is an amazing process! When I started doing it, I did not think so! I thought I would never accomplish anything, because of the hand of cards God gave me, and that was all I had. I just needed to deal with it and be happy with the way life was. The cards, keep in mind how I felt, I was nothing more than a simple guy with many big dreams. I never realized who I was! When I realized who I was, I understood this very clearly. I wanted to share this with everyone! The journey is the most incredible part! The journey of self-awareness and empowerment are the greatest gifts you will ever give yourself and your Soul!

Along this journey, your EGO may kick in with doubt, and you might fall into struggle within yourself. You may also get depressed, confused, upset, angry and end up experiencing emotions you want to run from. It is very important to follow your Soul through this process while experiencing these emotions. It is also very important to ask yourself "Why am experiencing what I am experiencing right now?" It is vitally important that you not ask yourself this question with the feeling of judgment. You must realize that these emotions are part of your human experience in the present moment! The self-judgment you will inflict on yourself will destroy your inner world more than you will ever imagine! Be gentle with yourself, love yourself, and know that everything you are going through is part of an experience.

> *Forgiveness is a virtue of the brave.*
> *Indira Gandhi*

Chapter 10
Forgiveness

One of the hardest concepts for me to grasp was forgiveness and to see things through the eyes of my EGO. It was really hard! My EGO felt forgiveness was a weakness. By forgiving; my EGO felt it gave someone permission to hurt me, or to act badly. Later, I learned that forgiveness was more for me than it was for other people. It was my way of letting go of the pain and anguish I had dwelling inside of me.

This element is vitally important to find peace inside ourselves. When we hold on and harbor anger inside, it sits and festers inside of us, potentially years and years. This kind of anger or intense emotion is what manifests mind poison later in life or in other situations.

I lost everything in my life I thought was important to me. This is how I learned to forgive. My EGO took a serious blow when I lost everything. It completely depleted my self-esteem. I sat there and felt like nothing, and blamed everyone else for where I was. I pretty much lived in the darkest hole I had ever been in. I cannot totally describe the anguish and pain I went through, but it was the worst feeling I ever had. I felt like nothing and a complete failure in life. I was not sure what I would do with my life without what was important to me before.

This is where we get caught up...at this point I did not realize the incredible gift which had just been granted to me.

Through this experience I gained a sense of clarity I never had before. It would send a ripple effect into the universe that would bring many lessons, teachers and people into my life to help me gain this clarity. Going forward; I set a goal to work for God. This meant that God was going to prepare me for that work.

One of the teachers who came to me was Jesus. Keep in mind that I was the person who grew up Christian and told God that I hated him because he hated me, when I was eighteen years old. I was angry that God had the nerve not to love me even when I did nothing wrong! I was angry with God because he allowed the teachers and ministers he put on the Earth to teach hate and anger. He allowed many aspects of my family to be broken. He allowed my mother to be heartbroken at a very young age by the separation of my Grandparents. How dare he let all of this happen! I sat in meditation December of 2007 very relaxed and peaceful. Suddenly I felt a warm presence come behind me and I felt its loving energy come over my body. A blissful feeling beyond anything I ever felt, came from deep within me. I said to this energy "Who are you?" I hear back, "You know who I am my friend. "I realized it was Jesus and replied, "Why are you here? I do not even like you!" I thought he was the representative of the Christian faith! He stated back with what felt like all the love of the universe,

"I am here to help you love me because when you love me, you will learn to love yourself."

I have experienced immense energy in my meditations, but nothing like this. When he said you will learn to love yourself, I felt my body twitch in excitement as if it had been waiting to hear this my whole life! I remember this as clear as day, because he told me my teachers were on their way to help me! He also showed me how we are all connected as light beings and even though I did not really understand what he was showing me at the time, it would become clear to me later.

I think the hardest thing for me to grasp was the fact Jesus came and talked to *me*. WOW! How could this be possible? My EGO tried to grasp onto it with a sense of entitlement but when I worked with his energy I could not help but feel a healing presence deep within me. I started to gain a sense of security within me. The love I started to find within myself and for HIM was amazing! I learned beyond any book that FEAR causes us to be clouded and LOVE keeps us in flow.

I learned about forgiveness, from a physical teacher, in the real world named Virginia Drake. Every step of the way I learned inside myself and from Jesus. Virginia validated for me or helped me gain an even deeper understanding of the information I received. She encouraged me without judgment to go within myself and understand my greatness. I remember one day I realized forgiveness was about letting the pain go and allowing yourself to move on in life and not be stuck in the past. This is also when I realized I was my most vicious critic. I judged myself and destroyed myself from the inside out. I had to forgive myself for all the things I thought I had done badly in my life. I also learned that there was no right or wrong but just experiences. Forgiveness was also about letting others go so they could move forward and experience *their* lives and *their* path without emotional attachments to me.

The vision I had, became clearer. We are all ONE and we are all connected. I actually saw what our human minds want to call a grid or matrix. I saw strands of light interconnected in geometric round shapes that went on for infinity. I also saw how my anger intertwined within the whole of this great grid of light and clogged up the grid. When I am angry with someone for what they did, I am unable to allow myself to be in flow with nature. I am totally restricted within myself. I have my back turned to the whole of consciousness. This basically works against the system and I saw this so deeply and profoundly it was almost too much for me to understand at first. When I am in a blocked state, the thoughts I have put a wrench in the system and I am resistant to the flow of all that is.

As I forgave myself and forgave others, I noticed the tension left my body and I gained an understanding of projection. On a deeper level I understood judgment. All these things kept me from really understanding how all this worked. It is hard to see things clearly; constantly distracted by judging others, worrying about what they are doing and not letting go of the pain inside. All of these things caused my reactions, and created the mind poison I wrote about.

Forgiveness forced me to let go of the tension and flow with the universe again. I was able to feel Love inside that I had never felt before. What made this really cool was that it came from my actions. The stronger I got in forgiveness and lived in the moment the more solid of a foundation I built. The happier I got, the more love I felt.

Let us take a second and practice this. Reading it does not make it happen inside of you. I want you to think about someone or even something you did that you have not let go of. Maybe a friend said something hurtful to you or you told a white lie as a child or something really BIG! Feel that feeling it gives you. Let the guilt swell up or the anger swell up inside you. Let the emotion build inside of you until you cannot take it anymore. Now stop. Wrap your arms around yourself and grab on tightly as if someone is hugging you. Say "I forgive you." out loud. Most importantly, I want you to say "I forgive you." inside yourself and allow yourself to let go and forgive yourself! Take a deep breath as you do this. Let your imagination take that feeling of forgiveness throughout your body and allow it to release any tension.

When you forgive or love another that is exactly what you are giving yourself. When you are angry with someone else that is exactly what you are giving to yourself. This is why self-awareness is key! The EGO does not understand until it learns to understand this. Remember the EGO's job is to protect you within this world so weakness, when it feels like a victim; is not an option. This is why loving your EGO and forgiving it is imperative. Getting up with it and not understanding what it is trying to do is only going to bring it deeper into its need to protect itself but is going to make it want to protect itself from you.

I changed my behavior by practicing the principles in this book. I continue to practice these principles each day. I bring all of this up in the chapter on forgiveness because as you practice the principles in this book you *will* fall on occasion and you *will* get out of balance on occasion. It will be very important for you to understand forgiveness because as you fall and start to self-judge yourself, it will be necessary for you to forgive yourself. Go deep within yourself; don't allow the self-judgment. Become aware of why you got out of balance. Love yourself in return for the opportunity to grow on the inside of you.

> *Where the soul is full of
> peace and joy, outward
> surrounding and
> circumstances are of
> comparatively little
> account.*
> *Hannah Whithall-Smith*

Chapter 11
Revelations of the Soul

So far, I have been writing about a set of principles or ideals I used to create peace within myself. Ultimately, my goal with this is to share it with others so they may be able to find peace within themselves. You may be asking "Well, this is all great but how did he do this? Where did he get all of these revelations and his information?" The answer to these questions came directly from my soul. As crazy as this may sound to some of you, this is how I achieved levels of peace in my life. This is how I was trained to do the things I do and how I am able to talk about the things I do today. I gained a Soul Education because I directly listened to the guidance of *my soul* and took advantage of the opportunities presented to me. I imagine it was like a bunch of puzzle pieces given to me piece by piece; eventually they came together which allowed me to see a bigger picture. During some periods, I became very frustrated and wondered why I could not get the whole picture/answer right away. I finally realized my soul has enough wisdom to know I would have rejected what it was trying to teach me because I was not ready to hear it.

It has been a beautiful process and a beautiful journey along the way. The journey is where all the excitement is and is where all the true rewards are found. My visitation by other spirit beings such as Jesus who taught me a such a vast amount. Because my mind thought of myself as being very small, I am just a regular guy with big dreams. Sometimes I still get caught up with the idea of speaking with Jesus. I even remembered a time when I made fun of people who stated they spoke to Jesus. It made me really understand about my judgment of others because that is how I judged myself. I tried to deny the fact *I* really experienced this. I even avoided telling people that I spoke to him and he guided me. What is amazing about this is that he speaks to all who will listen. I learned we all have this ability to speak to him and learn about compassion and how to love ourselves. I know it is because of the fear inside that we are unable to hear him and we do not *listen* to him. I listened. Without speaking words, he showed me how connected and interconnected we are. When we doubt we can communicate with him, we doubt the fact we are him. We are all part of a whole.

The most incredible part of this connection to a whole is having access to the wisdom of all that is. The catch is this; in order to access all the information, we have to get very still inside to receive it. Remember we have to have "ears" to hear the wisdom of God. We are congested when our minds race with outside thoughts. When we are in struggle, we will not be able to hear the wisdom of God. This is actually why meditation, prayer and study are so important. These are our times to connect back to our source. By not connecting we deny what we vitally need in order to have clarity and even to sustain life itself.

My time with Jesus helped me understand the beauty of who I am. He also taught me when I look at myself and belittle myself; it is my EGO measuring me against the rest of the world. I am not honestly looking through my soul's eyes or the eyes of God. My soul is beautiful beyond measure. My soul does not worry about the clothes I wear because the brightness of my soul does not need the latest fashion label. It is not concerned with the flashiness of my car. My soul knows who it is and tries to get me to see what it sees. Those feelings of belittling are what separate me from my soul.

When we do the work and go within ourselves we are waking up to who we are. We are allowing our soul to come back to life and be in oneness with us. We are marrying our soul to become ONE. One of the craziest parts is that I did not read many books or have very many physical teachers. I just followed the signs and learned how to listen. If someone handed me a book and I felt the need to pay attention to it, I would. Most of the time I would let my soul guide me to read what I needed and I used my everyday life to learn about who I am on a deeper level. Life is the higher education we are all looking for a "this is real life" experience! Look at life as a huge experiment. You are the scientist getting to try different experiments. Life is your big laboratory to test theories and learn from experiencing those theories. The trick is to sit back and watch as your soul guides you through the laboratory. This is important because if you fall into judgment, you will make decisions based on the EGO and not the path the soul knows is the highest and best for you. The EGO will make decisions based on FEAR if it is not in oneness with the soul. The EGO will tell you that things are bad for you, be mad at someone else and blame others. It will block the flow of life for you. The Soul *will* discern the right path for you based on what is in flow for the universe.

Most of us operate from a space of reacting to the world around us instead of being in flow with it. What I realized is the more and more I reacted to the world, the more and more I buried my soul and kept it from being in harmony with myself. You see, your reactions constrict your soul and stifle it. One day, in meditation, I realized that our judgments are a reaction, and we base our judgments on our previous experience; not on facts. This is where my journey with Jesus helped me so much because his words were "I am here to teach you to love me and when you learn to love me, you will learn to love yourself." This taught me what I give out to others is exactly what I am experiencing. The body knows no difference, it only knows it is feeling love.

This is why we should give love and see our enemies with love instead of with anger because of what it does to us physically. After I saw how interconnected we are spiritually, I realized the anger we harbor within us sends a ripple into the universe. I learned on a deeper level our thoughts and emotions are a vibrational frequency and when I send out anger, it causes more anger outside of me. These are not just fancy words in a book. I could feel it in my body traveling outward. This ripple was causing more anger with everything it contacted. THIS WAS HUGE! This meant in essence that we are like a big radio antenna. As we have thoughts, feel things and go through our days, we constantly create frequencies. I could feel it! I did not see this before because I was so busy doing other things in life and I worried about how I would get people to love me whom I could not hear! I did not have "ears" to hear or "eyes" to see what I was creating! This is the process we practice here on earth. I realized most people look at these things as magical or mumbo jumbo or even evil. The great part of where I am in life, I have learned from the spirit. I do not need to defend or debate what I know, I only have to live it to the best of my ability. I have to be that model. This was a hard lesson to learn because of the struggle going on inside of me.

Most of us want to debate what we know, or believe. We continue to debate and defend with others about *how* we believe. This is because we have a struggle and a debate still going on inside of us. What we do is debate with ourselves. Our mirror and what others mirror back, are the insecurities we have with our own belief system. If we have to defend something, then we are not strong in how we believe. If we were strong in how we believed, there would be no need to defend it. Our solid foundation in who we are and what we know would be strong enough; it would not need debate.

I had the realization all I have to do is live what I believe and speak my truth. I have to be confident in who I am and what

I believe. I have to be who I am, live it and walk the talk. If I do that, I will be living an empowered peaceful life. I will also empower others to live and believe what they want and what inspires their soul. When we live a life of confidence in flow with others, we allow them to be who they are. We allow ourselves to be who we are as well.

This to me was a profound concept, because it made me realize our world is backwards. This world does not teach us to allow others to be who they are. We learn in this world to follow the rules set by other human beings, to conform to their ideas of how things should be. In this lesson, my soul taught me we do not have to conform to assessments by others nor do we have to follow their rules. I realized people react based on life experiences. They filter things based on the experiences they had in life. This is why we FOLLOW OUR SOUL and not the words of a human being! Yes, there are times we listen because it rings true to our soul but in reality, we *are* listening to our soul, not the other person. What someone else says is lighting something up in you and your soul is letting you know.

Another thing I learned is when another soul or person is trying to point something out to you, it might not be time for you to hear the message trying being conveyed. However, what they are doing is planting a seed within your psyche and that seed will fully manifest and grow when it is ready. In other words, all things happen in divine timing and divine order. Needless to say, in our world the reason all of us are out of balance is we are trying to force divine order and bend it to the will of our EGO. What is interesting about this and what I learned the hard way is that when I try to force something it always ends up being a disaster. This is the very reason we are all bound up inside and full of tension. All of us are fighting *against* and resisting the natural order of things. We are always in opposition of something in the world. We further perpetuate the struggle within us. To me this is actually comical, because I look at my life and realize what I have done to myself inside. I just shake my head with a bit of a smile and realize I did not know what I was doing because I was unaware. I have been my own worst enemy working against my soul on such a vast level. As I did this I continued to bury myself deeper and deeper into a hole of darkness and could not see anything but my own depression and self-pity. Now that I look at it from a soul perspective and how easy life can really be, it takes on new meaning for me. It makes me smile to realize all the times I got upset inside and when I acted out, I was just being irrational.

We do not really know what we are doing to ourselves in life because we are not self-aware. We act in the capacity of our own comprehension, therefore; *that* is all we can expect of ourselves. When I find myself fall into old patterns I immediately realize what I am doing and it makes me laugh. It is a reminder of a place I do not want to revisit. It reminds me when we act in an irrational, un-awake manner how comical it can be. This is part of the great adventure I found. The SOUL wants to experience everything but not get distracted and lose sight of the beauty which is the soul.

One other powerful thing I realized, when people try to tell me something, or teach me something, it is not always the time for me to hear what they have to say. However, they have planted a seed within the psyche that will grow and fully manifest when the time is right. Again, things happen in divine timing and divine order. This is one of the reasons why I stopped doing typical psychic readings of the future. I stopped telling people how their lives will be in regards to love, money, family, health, etc.

Instead, what I choose to do is help people look at their filter, listen to their own inner voice, and ask themselves the vital question "Is this coming from FEAR or LOVE?" When they ask themselves this question, they will learn how to follow their own inner guidance and allow their soul to guide them. The misconceptions people have that only a few people are able to talk to God or have abilities to see things, are incorrect! There are not just a select few people in the world who have these gifts. WE ALL DO! No one person is greater than another. We are all

68

made in God's image! Some people have done more work and practice than others but we all have the same potential to be the brightest light possible. I have no problems with psychics, and on occasions I will ask my friends about what their intuition says. When I turn to a friend I feel strongly about that decision. I follow my inner voice which guides me to my friends. Their insight will take me down a path and I may make decisions based on the information given to me and as a result will lead me to new experiences.

Ask and it will be given to you; seek and you will find; knock and the door will be opened to you.
Jesus (Matthew 7:7)

Chapter 12
Learn To Ask and Receive

Not long after I started meditating, I started to hear Archangel Michael. It started one day when I was in meditation and I heard "If you do not ask, we cannot help you." I heard that over and over again and was stunned by the fact this was not a voice in my head. I asked people what they thought and of course, the friends I hung out with at the time thought I was crazy. There was a time I took too many drugs at a party and that was the point they thought I started hearing things. One day I asked a psychic friend of mine what I was hearing. She said it was an Angel or my spirit guide. I was still very new to this so I felt this was all crazy talk. I began studying metaphysics because my mother started going to a women's psychic group. I actually thought my mother was doing something pretty crazy because it made no sense to me. It could not be real, could it?

It was about as real as Christians who talk to God. What makes this so amazing is we all have the ability to do it. Most of us see ourselves as so small, it is not possible for us to comprehend this concept. Therefore, we stick to what we only see with our eyes or can prove with our logical mind. We are so scared to believe in something on faith alone. Again, this seriously limits and blocks the part of you that believes in things on faith. There are so many things we cannot see with our naked eyes. We believe a cell phone will send a signal from the handset and you can speak to someone across the world but we cannot believe that our thoughts create a vibration. If we tune ourselves to this, we can feel that vibration. I have spent all this time using science to prove what I already felt and learned from my spirit. I realized the more I looked for the proof, the more I missed the joys of discovery within me.

One day, I asked the spirit what its name is and to show itself. I actually got a sign about two weeks later but it took even longer for me to figure it out. One day I was in the mall looking for Christmas presents, I saw a necklace with a crystal sword in it. A radiant blue shined from the sword. I heard "This is me," in my head. I took it to mean I should get the necklace because it was pretty. I didn't realize it was a symbol. About four months later I was at a weekend retreat about *How to see our Angels* and I was wearing the sword necklace. Someone said to me "There is a radiant blue shining from the necklace."

I just dismissed what they said at first. I thought it was just the way the light hit it. This same person said "Wow, it just beams this blue light!"

I smiled and said, "Okay, well, thank you."

It was not until other people noticed the necklace was shining this blue light when my mother said the same thing. Then I said "This is really cool". The instructor said "You have the Archangel Michael around you and he is trying to talk to you."

It made me realize it was the Archangel Michael who was trying to teach me before when he said, "If you do not ask, we cannot help you."

From that point moving forward, *I asked*! Sometimes I felt like I received help and other times I felt the help I received was different than what I asked for. I realized and learned that sometimes we ask with our EGO and it goes against divine order. Sometimes we ask for what is in alignment with divine order. So, if that is the case, why should I ask? Why not just let divine order take you where you need to go? I struggled with this for a long time. Many times I would try not to ask but in

71

desperation, I would. When you are in a desperate moment it means you are asking with the limitations of your EGO.

One day I realized we have to experience being deprived of what we want because it humbles us. It reminds our EGO that we are a part of something greater than just this physical flesh. It is a part of the whole body of God, and if we received our wants based on the filter of our EGO, it would go against the grain of the WHOLE. The other part of this is that GOD prepares us for what we want by getting us emotionally ready for the things we dream. This is when I learned the journey is the exciting part. If we got the lover we always dreamed about without learning how to love ourselves, how could we ask that lover to love us, when we do not love ourselves?

You see, God prepares us for that lover before we actually have him. When we are at the point in divine timing and divine order to have that lover, it will happen. We will know what to say, how to say it, and be at the right place at the right time. All of this took me almost ten years to learn from the time Michael told me that you have to ask in order to receive help. It took me asking and getting upset and asking and being happy many times, for me to realize these experiences gave me the wisdom I needed.

Many years later, after I started talking to Michael, I had a lot of bad things happen to me. I felt like the world was caving in on me and I needed Michael to come around me again. In reality, he never left but he reminded me "If you don't ask, we cannot help you."

When this happened, I felt like I had asked but no one listened. I even went to the beach one night on a full moon and yelled at God that he was not helping me! It was funny because that night I heard "Well I have been trying to tell you, but you are not listening or acting upon the opportunities that were presented to you."

I am not going to lie, this is one of those points in my life where I actually laughed at myself again. I realized I was getting angry because of my fears about taking advantage of opportunities. I missed many paths along the way because I was afraid they might be the wrong path. Paralyzed by fear, I missed so many opportunities in life. I did not realize there really was no right or wrong path but each path has an experience for the SOUL. We spend too much of our lives missing things, and not enjoying life because we do not want to take the wrong path or make the wrong decision. We miss so much by worrying about what *is* the wrong path! What I have learned is, I go with the path I feel the greatest pull towards and I follow that path. When I feel FEAR I spend time processing it so I am able to understand FEAR and move on from that FEAR. The reality is that if I spent my whole life avoiding what I am afraid of, then I would not experience anything in life. Yes, there are times I go down one path and realize another would have been easier. If I had gone down that path, I would not have gained the wisdom I gained. This is why we want to eliminate the thoughts "I should have done it this way" or "I could have done it better this way." All paths have something to be gained.

I also learned from processing the words that Michael gave me, the many times he worked with me; indecision is FEAR and not proceeding forward in life stems from FEAR as well. If we are working in love and working from our SOUL then we will be standing in the flow of divine order and will not miss any opportunity that presents itself. We will know with divine wisdom what to do and not to do because our thoughts will just flow to us like a breeze within us.

I spent a great deal of my life *stagnant*, not making decisions because I was afraid of what I would lose. I did not stand up to the ones I felt could be my lovers or were my lovers because I was afraid they would leave and I did not want to lose them from my life. What I learned was I was holding myself back and enabling them by not standing up for myself and by not stating clearly what I wanted. If there is anything I learned through all of this it is this, if I am not clear about what I want with someone else then it is obvious I am not clear of what I truly want inside myself. How can I expect God or the universe to understand what I want if I am not even clear about what I want inside myself?

One of the reason I had so many failed relationships, is I was not clear about what I wanted for me. I was not able to clearly tell others what I wanted from them. The result was, fights between us because we both felt we were not getting what we wanted in life. Neither one of us knew ourselves nor who we were as individuals. We were unable to make clear what was needed to enhance the relationship and let it grow. Understanding yourself and getting deep into yourself is one of the most important parts of the process of growing spiritually to bring peace in your life. How can we know what we want when we do not even understand the first thing about ourselves? The answer: *it is not possible*. We continue forward blindly, knowing we want something, but think something is missing. We are unable to know what that something is because we have not taken the time to understand our needs. We are not operating from a balanced body, mind, and spirit. We need these to be in balance, to understand who we are.

Once we understand ourselves clearly from the body, mind and spirit; we begin to ask for things to manifest in our lives which seemingly come easier. We are now operating from the divineness of our soul. We have to listen to our soul, what it needs us to do, what path it needs us to take. We would not understand this unless we proceed forward and make mistakes along the way.

We do not gain the wisdom needed *unless* we fall down and hurt ourselves along the path. I would not be able to teach people unless I am able to talk from my experience! Otherwise, I would just be operating from words that I read, instead of the wisdom gained from experience. I would not overcome my FEARS unless I faced them head on, and understood them on a deeper level. These principles have to be practiced, and experienced, otherwise they are just pretty words on paper in a book. It is time to bring these words out of this book and start proceeding forward with your life and experiencing it.

The last lesson comes from when God advised me he was sending me the opportunities and I did not act on them. It was amazing because I never laughed so hard at myself. What I learned: Often times we are given a lot from God and people, but are unable to see what it is because we are so focused on other things. We are unable to appreciate what was given in the moment because of our EGO. This is vastly why we want to appreciate everything in our life at all times because that appreciation brings us more opportunities and greater things to experience.

Appreciation allows us to see the opportunities that come into our lives and see things on a greater scale. I realized many things I did on the inside of me by the hours spent processing my thoughts. It is amazing how we read all of these self-help books, but never realize all the information is built right inside of us. How do I know? Well I could say it was a great spirit who brought me this information. The reality is that my visitations from Archangel Michael, Jesus, Buddha and many other spirits and earthly teachers were all me! Yes, they are archetypes in our psyches. I have no doubt in my mind there was a Jesus and a Buddha in physical form. I also truly believe there was a Saint Michael. These beings brought me to a point in myself where I could see it within me. These spirits who are really me, and all of us, are all one. They guided me to the water so I could drink the cosmic water of wisdom and wash away all the doubt within me. I learned to understand and appreciate who I am. What is very apparent, as we learn how to ask and how to receive, we get to understand who we are and understand clearly what we want to ask and what we want to receive.

We have created a deception for ourselves. We are searching for something in life and continue to look around for what we want but in turn, have no idea what we want because we have no idea who we are. I know some of you are saying that you know exactly what you want in life! I am going to gently ask you this: Do you still experience anxiety, depression, disdain or anger? Are you experiencing any of the emotions, which keep you from experiencing the true love you are? The truth is if you have answered yes to any of these things, then at some level you do not fully understand who you are. I do not fully understand who I am, and I am still in the process of discovering me.

If I do not fully understand who I am, then how could I possibly know everything I want in life? In addition, if I do not fully understand everything I want in life, then how can I possibly create the life of joy I want, or appreciate it for what it is? The answer is to love the journey of discovery. Understand the process *is* the adventure. You look for tending and attention for yourself, but in order to get the attention, you have to love yourself along the journey. This is why we appreciate every moment we experience, because in turn we appreciate ourselves. We change the self-judgment inside of ourselves. When we change our inside world and appreciate who we are right now, we change this world. We will be a light unto the world, changing it from the inside out.

> *Let go. Why do you cling to pain? There is nothing you can do about the wrongs of yesterday. It is not yours to judge. Why hold on to the very thing which keeps you from hope and love?*
>
> *Leo Buscaglia*

Chapter 13
Letting Go and Letting God

I can honestly say that I was and can be very controlling. I know the very nature of our EGO within our current culture of limitations is to be controlling. We are raised and bred in a society and culture based on FEAR.

In fact, I do not know a person on this planet who does not have some amount of control issues or does not need some level of control in their lives. People have disagreed with me but when I watch them, I can see the level of control in their lives. It directly mirrors the control I have had in my life. Most of us miss the fact we need control so we can hold onto what we feel comfortable with. When we do not maintain order in our lives, or allow things to flow in the natural order of things, we fear what will come. I saw this level of control in many aspects of my life and all of it stemmed from fear. We can really go deep into this subject such as people being late to social events, work commitments or just being late. One day a light went off in my head when my friend was late for something we planned weeks in advance. I realized getting upset about it was not changing the fact my friend was late or helping either of us. In reality, getting upset was not helping the situation at all. It was only festering and manifesting more misery in the situation. I asked my friend why he was late and if it is a habit. I asked him what prevented him from being on time to pre-planned events. Usually people will spurt out excuses of why they were late with a defensive tone because they feel guilty. Why punish them when they already are punishing themselves? This is a person who is likely beating himself up on the inside a good majority of time. The main thing we want to observe in this situation is that he was probably hurting in all areas of his life.

Times like these, we need to speak our truths with compassion and remind them of the original planned start time and also listen and pay close attention to what they say. They will usually tell you without realizing it, why they were late. There is always a message behind the message. The most important lesson is to let go and let God. In this situation especially, we do not know the divine plan for this person and we certainly do not know the lessons they are going through. Their path is their path, and does not mean we should allow their path to hurt us or bring us down. It also means we should speak our truths when we feel strongly about it. In the end we let it go so they can go on their path to grow and learn the way they should.

This subject is a hard one to practice because we are living on the outside world and most of us are not paying attention to the inside world. We are so busy trying to help others and tell them what we think is best for them that we are not paying attention to what is going on inside of us. What is remarkable about this is that while my mother was sick in the hospital I noticed some people got upset because they felt the doctors should be handling her care differently. Even I got upset with how they were taking care of my mother until my friend Carol reminded me they were doing things to the best of their ability and really thought they were helping her. When she said this, I saw things as I needed to. God (all of consciousness) had a divine plan which was not visible to my EGO. My soul knew, but I was not paying attention to my soul; I was upset and crying. I was only paying attention to the limitations of my human emotions. Then, in an instant my spirit stepped in and reminded me that all things are divinely perfect. In that moment, I realized I had to let go of all expectations of the outcome, and just be in flow with the journey. I know you are sitting there saying that is very hard to do. A few years ago, I would have probably agreed with you but now I cannot imagine believing anything other than in divine timing and divine order.

This is where our peace comes from; letting go of control. We must allow ourselves to fall into the flow of life and just experience things as they come to us. We spend a great amount of our time worrying about what is going to happen, instead of what is happening now. My mom being sick was an extraordinary experience because I was able to let go of fear and experience letting go of the expectations. This is not to say I will not go back into fear, it might happen again depending on the circumstances but this is all a part of the journey. This part makes all of our experiences rich and exciting. Most of us avoid these feelings because we think it is not very spiritual to fall into fear. If we do, it is because we are human and a spiritual being having a human experience. We want to go back and look at the emotions we are experiencing so that we can become aware of why we experienced them. Was it FEAR or was it LOVE? In order to do this, I need to allow the flow of God to do what it does best; create!

There are stories after stories of people experiencing something in life where they had to let go of something in order to let it be. A saying I remember "Let them go and if they were yours in the first place then they will come back and if not then they were never yours." This admittedly was a challenge for me. In my mind, especially in romantic relationships; I felt I needed to give my all in order to keep it going. I was correct! When it was time for a relationship to end or transition into something different; no amount of trying to love them more or do more for them would change the fact the relationship needed to change or end. Sometimes people are not meant to be together on that level. Sometimes it is not the right timing for them to be together on that level. What is very important is to allow your heart to guide you in this type of situation. My last long term relationship had lasted several years. Several years were spent in a long distance relationship with us breaking up and getting back together. We wanted something out of that relationship but were unwilling to make the step forward to make it happen. In reality neither one of us was willing to trust enough to take a risk on the other. He did not want to move where I lived and I did not want to move where he lived. We spent years traveling back and forth and being alone when we had to leave each other; never really bringing the relationship to the level it needed to be for us to have that deep connection. We were both codependent, just filling the void of eachother's need to be with someone. Neither one happy with who we were as an individual and in the end, we both hurt each other and created a very upsetting break up. This is when I really started to look at and ask myself the hard question and when I really started to practice awareness and understanding who Jeremy was! The break up, when I really look at it; was a blessing! Since then people have mentioned him and his life is going places, meeting the goals he always wanted. Our paths were changing and our lives were going in different directions. Everything is divinely perfect, but if either one of us would have let go earlier and just allowed the flow of God to work through us; we would have probably saved ourselves a lot of pain and suffering. This experience has taught me how to recognize when I am taking myself down a path of suffering even faster so I can practice my principles of self-awareness and eventually self-acceptance.

All of this started because I declared I was willing to follow God. God wanted to help me all along but was just waiting for me to ask for help. God came to help me understand who I was. The process had to happen. I had to first say yes, and experience all of my emotions along the way. Several experiences later there were a whole array of emotions. I experienced all of these because each time it gave me a greater understanding of why and what these emotions truly were. Each time my faith and belief in myself got stronger and each time my faith and belief in God got stronger. Now I know that *I am God*. Not in the sense that I am better than anyone else, I just know that I am a part of the greatest being there is: God! I am a physical manifestation, just a cell within the whole body of God. As a spirit (soul), I am in flow with all that is. As beings, we can bring everything into the flow just by letting go and allowing things to be. It is our FEAR that makes us want to control the world around us and it is our FEAR that says things should be a certain way. When we are in flow, we will not need to worry about the rules, because we will be in alignment with what is correct and what is not correct. We will have the answers of what is right for us and what is not right for us. Our EGO has the need to create our structure, when God already has a structure of the way things need to be. Our solid foundation is built on knowing all things are being taken care of. Our EGO turns our back on this foundation because it has the need to question everything.

What I have grown to understand is that as soon as I question things or try to figure them out, I am taking myself out of balance. When I let it go and let "God" then all things become possible. I know some of you are thinking you need to have dreams and goals. There is nothing wrong with dreaming or asking for things in life. Letting go and letting God does not mean you give up the excitement of creating goals and accomplishing them. What it means is that you are not attached with your EGO to the outcome. Do not be so set in stone that you miss the opportunities being presented to you right now in the moment. Recently, I had a dream that I owned twenty acres of land with several houses on the property. There was a radio studio for my radio show along with a television studio to produce television content. I had this great vision in my mind of how it was supposed to look.

Recently, my friend who is also my landlord advised me she had a house and land sitting empty and they needed work. She needed help! It made my mind laugh, because I thought, "Why not create it into something?" It made me really flow with ideas because she had very similar ideas. When we added everything there were five homes of friends as well as people who wanted to have gardens in their yards to produce food. My group of friends had the idea to have organic food and eat healthier for a long time. I had all the land I needed and even a potential space to have a radio studio, a place to have workshops, retreats, spiritual groups and a place to produce television content. I just needed to answer the call of opportunity and feel if it was in alignment with my heart. Was this my grand vision? Was this the land I wanted? Actually, to answer your questions, yes it had everything I wanted because the underlying theme of what I wanted was a group of people in flow with each other, creating a better tomorrow because we are having a better today. My vision was manifesting right before my very eyes! If I had been stuck on the idea of how I wanted it to be in every detail, I may have missed what was happening in front of my very eyes! I would not have been able to experience the gratitude of seeing it unfold before me. The truth is I might still see that twenty acres of land in one place, but I want to enjoy what I am seeing right now! This is God working, and why miss creation in its process?

The lesson here is to look again at everything you are doing and become self-aware. Do not to take this book and start criticizing yourself based on what you think you should be doing. Take the information in this book as a guide. More importantly, allow these words to open up your heart enough so you can follow your heart.

> *Great spirits have always encountered violent opposition from mediocre minds.*
>
> *Albert Einstein*

Chapter 14
Vibrations

This is where it all happens, through our vibrations as beings. I had an intimate look at this through a series of deep meditations. I saw bands of light all around, forming spherical shapes that created all that is around. The light emanated from the trees, water, buildings, cars, people, animals, etc. This is the basis of everything. I remember asking people what they thought this was.

Finally, one day I asked a friend who has a degree in physics. She said it was cool and sounded like a light vibration. She explained that pure light is a faster vibration than an area that is dark. She could probably explain this a whole lot better based on science than I can but this is what I understood after I processed it. We, as spiritual beings living in a human body having a human experience, live in a dark (dense) state. We live in slower vibration than the sun. The sun, having a very high vibration, is the brightest light in our solar system, supplying us with life on this planet. Without the sun we would not have plants growing as they should and would not get the vitamins and nutrients, we need from the sun to sustain our lives and we would not have many other things the sun provides.

What I have learned in my healing work is when we let go and let the flow of God work with us, that energy is pure love and pure love is the fastest vibration there is within the universe. The more we let go of FEAR, the faster our vibration become. After I realized this, a whole flood of information from scientific research came to me. This information helped me change my paradigm of how I see the world. I was no longer this flesh being who could not change anything; I was a spiritual being who could change my life by coming back into balance. The way to do this was by living and understanding the love within me will change me from the inside out. Now, we have already talked about how our body stores memories throughout the body and when we become aware of these memories and release the blocks; we transmute those memories back into love. This is what brings us back into *flow*. In flow, we are able to freely give love, and freely receive love. We have to have both to maintain a happy loving life of joy and peace.

To demonstrate this, I want you to stop for a few minutes. Take a deep breath in and then exhale out. Make sure to breathe in through your nose and out through your nose. Deep breathe in again and then out but this time I want you to stand for a second. Stand with your feet about shoulder length apart. Keep breathing the same way but say in your mind, not with your lips "CONNECT." I want you to visualize light pouring from the heavens down into your body, all the way down into your heart and then I want you to say in your mind "GROUND." Allow that energy to flow up into your heart. Lastly, I want you to say "BALANCE."

When you do this, I want you to allow yourself to balance between these two energies. You might feel your body wanting to pull slightly forward or backwards. It may want to sway around and move from side to side. Just let it. This is what is called being in the flow of divine energy. Now, I want you to allow yourself to feel love coming into you from God and allow yourself to receive it. Pay close attention to what your body does. Does it fall even more into flow or does it twitch? Does it relax or have more anxiety? This is where you will be able to tell how well you receive love. This is where we start processing why, and how we receive love so we know what we need to work on in our lives. Our body is programmed with memories we have and everything we ever felt in our lives is stored within our bodies.

Traumatic memories, sadness, depression, anxiety; all stemming from FEAR, create blocks of flow within the body and lower the vibration of the person. This is what the Chinese would call stagnant "Qi." This was explained in Chapter 7 but I wanted to touch on it again because we talked in detail about vibration.

How does vibration play into a peaceful life you ask? Simply said, this is a high vibration no disease can hold. Toxins cannot hold it within the body and massive healing can take place within the body. Remember, the higher the vibration the brighter the light. Light; to me, comes from a deeper level of awareness and that awareness leads us to the ultimate self-love. Love, being the highest vibration within the universe; heals all things. This is what Jesus did, he healed people through his compassion. He found that compassion. He realized fully who he was a beautiful child of God. He was self-realized!

We change our world by understanding ourselves as individuals and by doing so we are able to look at the world differently. We are able to approach the world with an inner strength built with a foundation of love. We already know, our individual world will change and the people around us will change. New people experiencing the same things we are experiencing will come into our lives. In other words; not only will we find love in ourselves but also people who are more loving will come around us. We not only change our paradigm but we change our reality.

> *What we are today comes from our thoughts of yesterday, and our present thoughts build our life of tomorrow: Our life is the creation of our mind.*
>
> *The Buddha*

Chapter 15
Manifesting Your World

What we are in search of is how to change our world and gain all our dreams! I saved this part for the back of the book, because I felt you needed to understand about who you are before you can effectively create the world around you. First, let me say you are always creating. There is not a time when you are not creating the experiences of each day, attracting the people in your life around you. That is all you! We, as beings, created in the image of God, means we were given the abilities of God. As we have discussed before, we are actually a part of the wholeness of God. By knowing this and understanding the very fact you are creating at all times, means you have to take full responsibility for your life. There is nothing within this world you have not created. I am going to stretch your mind for a bit to talk about how you have created everything in your world and also how god created it.

We have discussed before, we are a part of God. We have also talked about the fact that we have God's abilities. We should accept and take responsibility for all things around us. We should not blame anyone for how our lives are going and how the world is. I have brought this point to a great many people and it is a very hard pill to swallow when we think about how bad the world is. People fascinate me when they are all about how they create their whole world *when it rocks*! When people are complaining about wars, how toxic our food is and how horrible we treat our planet; I remind them they created it. They turn their back on that idea, saying it was not them, it was irresponsible and greedy people in the world who created it. This is not meant to pick on anybody or judge them. I did the same thing in my life, and this was one of those times I realized I had one finger pointing in judgment with three pointing back at me. I asked myself "When have I ever been irresponsible?"

I stopped and thought about the times I forgot to pay a bill on time, the times I missed calling someone on their birthday or not keeping my promise to someone, because I was too sidetracked with everything else going on in my life. I realized it was because I was out of balance and therefore unable to focus on what was going on around me. It was very hard for me at these times to see anything other than my own problems. To go even further, it really hit home when I was scared I would not have enough money. I would hold onto money to make sure I had enough to pay my bills even though I knew there was enough. I just had trouble letting go of it. I did not realize this was a form of greed. Greed is the desire to acquire more than what you need in material wealth or possessions. This need stems from the ideal we do not have enough money or material objects and we have to continue to gain more stuff. So really, greed is FEAR of not having enough. The people we judge and say are greedy are just as scared as we are. That type of FEAR is every bit as toxic as the toxic food we eat. We need to realize that we as a culture are addicted to toxic situations. As an observer, I have found a great deal of this comes from our need to get everything done as soon as possible or right now! We feel that we do not have enough time. However, we as souls have infinite amounts of time.

The real sense of awareness came when I started to understand how truly toxic I was and how it was coming from my fear I still had inside of myself. It became very apparent that we are all in the same boat. As we continue to have these fears and interact with others and their fears, we continue to create fear between all of us. Wars come from the need to control another's free will and path. Greed festers in all of us. Until we realize the abundance we have, it will continue to fester within all of us, continuing to create strife within the whole of consciousness.

What really opened my eyes was when I realized we only need just enough to fulfill all our needs. Those needs, as defined by our soul; allow us to live within alignment with our souls. Our souls do not need a massive amount of surplus sitting in the bank just so we feel safe and secure having it there. That type of safety and security is not based on a foundation of rock.

Some of you may be thinking I am saying it is bad to be rich. I am actually not saying that at all. Look at what you need for comfort to be in alignment with your soul. Your soul knows what that comfort level is. If your comfort level feels like one million dollars in the bank and it feels right with your soul then do it. Some people move from place to place and usually have enough money to get to where they are going. Once they get to their destination, they need to earn more money to move on to the next place they want to travel. There are also people who live in large houses with tons of money. Some have told me they do not feel comfortable in their own home and it feels like it is too much. What is the point of me telling you about this? Very simply, be true to yourself and be true to your soul. The soul knows what experiences it needs to grow and expand its awareness. The soul knows what is best for you and your life and it knows how to guide you each step of the way, so trust it. This is why the first part of this book is about understanding yourself and going into an inner journey to gain that understanding. If you have that understanding, all the rest falls into place.

Once we read about the Law of Attraction we try to manifest and create our world based on what we think we want feeling it is what the world is dictating. This is not following our soul, it is following what we think we want based on others' experiences. This is what gets us stuck, because it is not in flow with God. I even know televangelists who teach "By giving tithe, you will reap what you sow." When you give with the pureness of your heart, you will receive back tenfold. However, just because we hear ministers tell stories about people who receive millions of dollars as they gave out, does not mean you should expect the Benjamins to come back tenfold. There is nothing wrong with giving out and getting back money tenfold but the rewards may come back to you in another form, not necessarily in money. As we give out, we should give with no expectation of return. When it does return we should be willing to receive it. Just know as we give out, we invest in the wholeness of us (all consciousness). Giving with the pureness of heart means what we give out, we will always receive back in some form. Giving out love with love in our hearts, we will receive love back. Give freely of our heart with a wholehearted compassion, we will get back compassion in some form. The return may come when we least expect it. The rewards are there when we live in flow and expect a life of miracles. Keep in mind, it is all about the intentions you put forth and the feelings inside of you.

Remember when manifesting through EGO, our EGO is out of balance because it is not taking into consideration our SOUL. When we are manifesting through our EGO it will never bring a feeling of wholeness within ourselves because we forgot to include "the whole" in the manifestation. It is like a marriage; if a husband buys houses, cars and makes decisions for him and his wife, it is not congruent with what a marriage is all about. A marriage should be a partnership. He did not include his partner in the marriage, he just made decisions without her. The same thing happens with the mind, body and spirit. When they are not working together or we forget about one of the three components. The neglect of one will bring down the whole. When we only live with our EGO or what we logically see with our physical eyes, then we neglect the other aspects of who we are. Just like the spouse who felt neglected or not included, eventually they will have a diminished sense of self-worth and it will create an unhealthy relationship.

So manifest with a healthy relationship between the body, mind and spirit. This creates a world built on a solid foundation of mutual love and respect which will radiate out from you into the oneness of consciousness. It will bring even more harmony, peace and love to the world. This foundation is so important. There are many wonderful manifestors out there who have achieved a great deal of success within the world of man but because they did not build their solid foundation, something always seems to happen to them on some level. They do not feel fulfilled within themselves, their health continues to suffer or they eventually lose it all.

I have grown to appreciate there is more than my physical manifestation in the equation. Because of this, I humbly ask things like "Would it not be nice to have a vacation to Miami?" I add onto that "If it is in my divine plan, then bring it to me in divine timing and divine order; make it easy." I do not want to do it hard anymore. If it is hard, it is because I am making it hard. Once I say this, I let it go! I do not dwell on it and I do not keep thinking about it repeatedly. If it comes back in my thoughts, I repeat, "If it is my divine plan, then bring it to me in divine timing and divine order and make it easy." I have studied a lot of different faiths, prayer, witchcraft, universal law, and the basis of all the faiths is when you ask God for something, you ask and "LET IT GO."

Our EGO wants to grab onto what it desires, and desperately hold onto it hoping it will happen with the EGO's limited expectations. It wants to live in a safe little box and only experience life when it feels safe. Some of you feel you push yourselves to your limits all the time to overcome your fears. If you are still feeling pain, anxiety, stress, sickness, doubt or any of that, then you still have FEAR breeding within you. I look at it this way: as we face our FEARS, and become aware of them, it expands our awareness. As we dive more into the unknown of ourselves, we gain a higher vibrational perspective on life and how spirit works. This to me is exciting!

A gentleman once told me he was not afraid of anything. I later saw him complain about the world and how horrible it is. He spoke about how his family was terrible, his job was terrible and he was never going to get anywhere in life because people were working against him. I spoke to him, "You are upset about a great deal of things in this life." I suggested "You must be afraid of something." Simply put, misery breeds more misery. He was creating more misery in his life.

This subject is literally so deep we could go on and on with story after story of how to stay in alignment with our Soul and manifest the world we truly desire. This book is just a guide to help you look within yourself, and really start to listen to that inner voice, so you can hear the call of your soul. One thing I challenged myself to do, was to look at my intentions of what I was thinking, what my emotions were and what I was intending on a deeper level.

Let us recap our text so far so that we can get a clear picture on how to manifest our lives in this moment.

1. Begin a process of your inner journey so you can become more self-aware.

2. Understand, in stillness our goals manifest faster, because we are not full of chaos of thoughts. We are in balance and have a clear understanding of who we are, because we are in oneness with our body, mind and spirit.

3. Set your intentions on a life of happiness and a world of miracles, do not just wish for them (know they are coming).

4. Flood your thoughts with thoughts of joy, happiness, abundance, love, peace and anything that brings you into a higher vibration.

5. Process the negative thoughts and find the base FEAR so you can release that block.

6. Pay attention to your intentions. If you want to find a relationship based on mutual respect and love, know you need to give yourself mutual respect and love in order to manifest that into your life. Otherwise, you will find a different journey.

7. Know God will bring you exactly where you need to be right now in this moment. If you want love and you still think very little of yourself on the inside and basically do not feel worthy of love, God will bring you someone to help you understand that in yourself.

8. Play with this, enjoy this and start to ask for your goals and desires, but have no set expectations on how it will look, when it will be, or how it will be.

9. Remember, you already are abundant because you are a child of God. Right now, in this moment, you already have everything you need. We are manifesting for the joys of manifesting and for the experience, not because we lack anything.

10. Let it go and put it in a higher power than your physical manifestation. Manifest with your Soul.

11. Remember to ask for things to happen, "In your divine plan, in divine timing and divine order." Always make it easy! Why do it hard?

12. Be grateful for all of your manifestations, because they are all equally beautiful.

The one thing I can say is this is not difficult. We make it difficult, because our EGO wants to grab onto a process someone else had success with, and hold that into a dogmatic idea. The points I give above are just for your reference, but remember to follow your heart. It will always know the highest and best path for you.

The last point on the subject of manifestation is this: remember that you are a child of God, Divine Royalty. You do not have to play it small. Jewelry, castles, cars, or money do not make you grand. The lightness of your heart makes you a BEAUTIFUL and RADIANT child of God.

> *It's the repetition of*
> *affirmations that leads to*
> *belief. And once that belief*
> *becomes a deep conviction,*
> *things begin to happen.*
> *Claude M. Bristol*

Chapter 16
Affirmations

When someone first brought up the idea of affirmations, I thought they were kidding me. I thought it was crazy. I tried to understand how saying these daily affirmations would help me change my life. One day my mother used the affirmation "I am whole, healthy and perfect." I realized how powerful the words were. When I saw her using this affirmation, I started to use it myself. At one point, I said it repeatedly in my mind and flooded my thoughts with this affirmation. A shift in my body happened.

I was so rejuvenated on energy from the positive feelings I gained towards myself. It was incredibly blissful but at one point I actually got a headache. How could I get a headache when I was doing something so positive? The self-judgment, self-doubt, self-criticisms and general negative feelings I had in my mind and body were replaced with thoughts of love and positive statements. It was foreign inside of me. This type of change within us comes with growing pains of the spirit. What I did was reprogram my mind, body and spirit.

Remember at the beginning when I talked about how we stored our thoughts and feelings all over our body. All of these memories and thoughts create our programming and we can change our programming at any time through a process of letting go of fear and transmuting it into love. One of those steps is affirmations. I have found affirmations effective at moments when I could not think of a positive thought for the day. Times when I could not find gratitude in my heart and all I could think about was what was bad with the world, I thought of an affirmation. I just started reciting to myself with my inside voice and not my vocal chords; how perfect I was and how perfect the world was. What I found was the time I spent doing my affirmations allowed me to switch my mindset so I could take the time to process the FEAR going on inside me. Our FEAR that dwells within in us is the programming which causes the diseases within our body. The affirmations provide us an avenue to help assist in reprogramming our bodies. Ultimately, it is still very important to dive deep down inside ourselves. It allows us to look at all of the false programs that keep us from having happy and joyful lives.

The idea behind affirmations is to allow yourself to find the affirmations you need. They can surface in your thoughts, as your body needs them. Your soul and body will tell you what you will need and this will come through your inner voice. It can also come in the form of a book given to you or any text that inspired you to create an affirmation. When I heard my mother use the affirmations, it was exactly what I needed at that time. I have used many other affirmations since then to help me in my journey. I am going to list a few here to help you with your journey.

1. I am whole, healthy and perfect.

2. I am abundant in all things and all things come to me in divine timing and divine order.

3. I have everything I need in the time I need it. I am lacking nothing.

4. I am perfect love and I have a perfect relationship with myself and others.

5. I am divine royalty and all things flow to me easily and freely.

6. I am pure love and all things around me manifest in perfect love.

These are just a few but I found them massively helpful. I can honestly say this helped me develop a deeper relationship with myself. It also allowed me to change how I felt about myself.

It is powerful to do these affirmations gazing at yourself in the mirror looking into your own eyes. By doing this; you are directly speaking with your soul and facing yourself, giving yourself the attention you have always desired. Developing a relationship with oneself is a part of the process of finding inner peace. When we can have that solid relationship with ourselves. We are developing what our inner spirit truly wants. This is the path of the soul.

Another thing I did was stand in front of the mirror and spend time looking at the physical things I did not like about myself. I took time to point out the things I love about myself. I found something to be grateful about even in the parts of myself I did not want to love. This was powerful for me. I had been doing this for a very long time and one day I watched a video of myself speaking and I realized how beautiful I was. It made me smile. For many years I had found myself unattractive and I did not think I was even a good speaker or teacher. What that moment did for me was help me realize I was happy about what I was saying and I was happy about the person on that camera. This was a huge shift for me. I realized all the inner work I had done inside myself paid off. I found an inner peace. All the things I taught to this point had become second nature for me. It was an epiphany how happy I was. I looked at everyone around me and realized I had loving people around me. It was a very good place to be.

A human being is a part of a whole, called by us the Universe, a part limited in time and space. He experiences himself, his thoughts, and feelings, as something separated from the rest a kind of optical delusion of his consciousness. This delusion is a kind of prison for us, restricting us to our personal desires and to affection for a few persons nearest to us. Our task must be to free ourselves from this prison by widening our circles of compassion to embrace all living creatures and the whole of nature in its beauty.

Albert Einstein

Chapter 17
Retrieving Our Soul Fragments

Soul fragments are a subject I struggled with for a long time. It seemed so ridiculous to me that I had a fragment out there in the universe somewhere. It finally hit me one day when I was doing mirror work with myself, looking into my eyes; trying to understand an emotion that I was experiencing in that moment I gained an understanding about what a fragment was. I was looking in my eyes and the current emotion was pointing blame at another person for my hurt feelings. I realized I was giving that person power over me. I was discovering how powerful pointing a finger at someone else was. I realized I was giving them a piece of *me*. When I look at them and blame them for whatever I am going through, I lose a piece of myself. It fragments who I am instead of bringing it back to me to understand the full experience I am going through internally. This very habit is what creates karmic debt for the soul; it will continue to come back to us in several lifetimes ahead. This happens when we make ourselves less important than another. We go against our soul even though we know the path it wants to be on.

Through this process of learning, I realized that Karma is self-created. When we have something, we cannot let go of, or forgive within our self, we carry this with us into spirit. This continues to cycle repeatedly covering the same lessons throughout each life until we simply just let go of what we are holding onto.

This very lesson was demonstrated to me as I was in the middle of writing this book. During this time, my mother transitioned out of her body into her spiritual life beyond. She passed away and let go of the life she called Laurie McDonald and transcended into spirit. My mother knew she was loved, she had no regrets and she was proud of her life. She told me these things as she was dying. These words rang with me so intensely, they went deep into my soul. I realized she had released all of the things that held back her soul from transitioning into whatever it needed to be for her soul's journey. If she had not released what she needed to do, then she might have had to come back and experience it all over again. On her deathbed, she had become whole within her spirit. Even though her physical body was very ill, her soul embodied what it needed to move on. This very fact was demonstrated in 2009 when she had a heart attack. Through this, she had a near death experience. During her experience she had remembered that she needed to come back because she and I had more work to do. She was right! During that two-year period, she and I let go of the codependency we had between us and she spent the two years releasing things she needed to for her soul to heal. What I realize now, is that she was calling back her fragments so she could transition back into spirit as a whole spirit. She, as the constant teacher; was teaching me and many others, again in spirit.

In the next lesson that came, she confirmed what the Buddha taught me when he visited me years ago. He showed me we are all ONE and because we are all one, when we blame, shame or do not take responsibility; we are separating ourselves from the WHOLE of consciousness. This was what she taught me as well. She showed me on a much deeper level, the fluid motion of the universe. It flows like the ocean waves. When we flow in oneness, we live the most tranquil, peaceful and loving life. We no longer live in this state of resistance; we are now in the divine flow of the universe. One day I asked my higher self to show me how to be fluid inside so I could experience being fluid with all that there is. What I felt was the energy in me pushing out, and losing itself into the massive space we call God. I was no longer in this body, but my body was in what was all of me. This was what my mother was trying to show me in spirit. She said the personality that was Laurie is now back in the wholeness of spirit. Further, she said she is now part of all experiences of all souls, just the same as all of us are. She reminded me because we are all ONE, we are all a part of the same God (consciousness). It does not matter if we are Christian, Pagan, Buddhist, Black, White, Gay, Straight or any of our limited labels. We are all children of the greater whole. We are all Jesus, Buddha, Black, White, Christian, Pagan, Gay or Straight because we are all experiencing these labels through the collective whole. This is why all of our limitations of the EGO and our FEARS separate us and our judgments. They prevent us from becoming aware of who we are fully and prevent our souls from coming back to our SOURCE of creation.

Our separation is our SIN. The limitations of our EGO and our FEARS turn our back on the WHOLE that is SPIRIT. We are greater than any of us can ever imagine. Our rules of the way others should act are what keeps us from experiencing who we are to our fullest. Our sense of smallness fragment us and compact us into tiny little bodies of flesh we think our souls reside in. The reality is, our souls are so massive and so great; they are too great for our EGOs to handle.

There are many, many scenarios where we fragment who we are as beings. Any time you put your faith in something separate from yourself, you separate yourself from who you are. God is within you and all around you, not separate from you, so you put your faith in you as a whole. When you have faith in a separate being who sits on a throne, you are not seeing who God truly is: **EVERYTHING!** This is why we get still within ourselves so we can feel the beat and the waves of all that we are.

Every belief system, every judgment, every fear, everything that keeps you from feeling the tremendous warmth of love deep within you, is separating you from the whole of you, and this is fragmenting you. Through my path, I have studied many things but until I started the process of learning who I am on a deeper level, everything I read and learned still felt like it had a sense of separation and this is because I felt separate in me. I did not feel whole with myself and because of this, everything around me felt separate as if it was working against me. This is why we start the process I have outlined in this book. This is why we listen to our inner voice and allow it to guide us to liberation and freedom.

> *God created the law of free will, and God created the law of cause and effect. And he himself will not violate these laws. We need to be thinking less in terms of what God did and more in terms of whether or not we are following those laws.*
> *Marianne Williamson*

Chapter 18
Free Will

I have had tons of discussions about free will. We have the freedom to choose whatever path we want to take and no path is right or wrong. We can take a path where we feel love emanating from and our world will manifest love, abundance and all the things we desire or we can make a choice to live in resistance which will bring us more heartache, pain, or suffering. When we feel separated from God and separated from everything else. This thought process makes us feel like God above is punishing us. We feel this punishment because in reality we are punishing ourselves and cutting ourselves off from the Source who brings us joy and is the highest aspect of who we are.

We spend all our lives looking for acceptance from others around us and spend all this time believing God or others can never accept us. We need to realize we *are* accepted now! The people around us who say they do not accept us do not accept themselves. As we have discussed, they are not looking at what is mirrored back to them. They chose a life of judgment and resistance and I can guarantee they are experiencing that very same thing in their lives. A part of them is trying so hard to be accepted but that part still does not feel the love it so desperately desires.

Our true free will comes from allowing ourselves to be in flow with the whole of who we are. It comes from self-awareness. Free will comes when we have ended the struggle inside of ourselves. When we liberate ourselves from the self-made prison, we will create freedom for ourselves. At this level, we are free from all of our bonds, our attachments which hold us back and we are free of our belief systems that hold us in a prison of doubt based on the dogma we have created within ourselves.

Within God, there is the freedom to create at a higher level but in our human limitations; we imprison ourselves because we cannot see clearly. We cannot see that the things we do create a life of limitations. We are unable to see that when we label something we have limited it to that label.

When we say we are human, we are limiting the spirit to this human body. When we declare it is God, we allow it to go into flow with its source. We allow it to flow with itself and we allow it to experience love on a new level. This is the true path of the EGO. Learn to trust and let go.

Our EGO is what stifles our free will; not God. We prevent ourselves from having the things we want to be happy. We believe our love comes from outside of us when it comes from the richness of who we are on a spiritual level.

This is why stillness is so important. Being still and letting go of our mind chatter, allows us to feel the fluid motion of the universe. We are able to breathe the essence of God within us and allow the essence of God in us to come back to life. Our death is not our ending, it is our beginning of LIFE. This is why clearing our belief systems, hang-ups, anger and dogma is so important before we leave this physical manifestation. This allows us to pass into spirit and be free from the bonds of this earth. When we do this, we allow ourselves to come and go from this earth freely. We then become cosmic like the other ascended masters, such as Jesus, Buddha and many others.

> *You should know (God) without image, unmediated and without likeness. But if I am to know God without mediation in such a way, then "I" must become "he," and "he" must become "I". More precisely I say: God must become me and I must become God, so entirely one that "he" and this "I" become one "is" and act in this "isness" as one, for this "he" and this "I," that is God and the soul, are very fruitful as we eternally do one work.*
>
> *Meister Eckhart*

Chapter 19
Declare and Know Who You Are!

One thing I have definitely realized through my soul journey is the universe moves easily for one who is confident but also humble. This is well said in the book of Matthew 5:5 (NIV) "Blessed are the Meek, for they will inherit the earth." Let us take a moment to review this because meek does not mean weak. The times I worked with the Archangel Michael I knew this spiritual being was strong but also had a strong sense of peacefulness around his essence. To me, meek meant someone who was self-realized and had ended the struggle within himself. In this case, Michael had no battle going on inside of him and I felt his presence as he worked with me. This same presence was around

Jesus, Buddha and even the spirit of my mother. These beings lived in spirit but I have felt this presence in all of us at times. In this human existence, meek means the same thing. For us, when we fall into our EGO, we just use this as an opportunity to grow but we change our times of EGO very fast, because we KNOW who we are!

I found the meanings of words we use are not the original intent of the words. *To be humble* does not mean that one is insignificant; it actually means one that is very strong inside and strong in LOVE.

The key to all of this is LOVE! People that are meek and humble are peaceful and strong within themselves, with Love and in essence.

A person who is peaceful, with no struggle in themselves, is the meek and shall inherit the earth, because the kingdom of God opens to them freely. The person who is humble has built a solid foundation on rock within themselves. That foundation is built with bricks made of LOVE. They have built this inner strength of PEACE and LOVE for themselves and other people want to follow them and be around them because that is what they want for themselves as well.

It is the self-realized person who will want to empower the people around them, so they are able to experience the new world of LOVE within themselves as well. They are in their hearts, naturally they will emanate this to others.

How does this work? How do you get to this level of consciousness? To start, you want to practice the principles of following your heart and letting your soul guide you in life. This is your connection to God (source) and you will want to declare, and know who you are. This is foreign to some people because to declare you are of God and therefore are God, is a big step. Remember you are not saying this with a big EGO, you are saying this with a humble and meek heart. You will be saying it with strength of love in your heart. This is powerful! With this level of strength, you will be saying to God you want to remember you are his child. You want to come home and be at

ONE with all that is. This is what it means to walk and talk with God because you now love yourself by knowing who you are.

You are saying that this cannot happen overnight. I agree with you. What you are also saying is it is time for the world to start manifesting for you and creating a world of awareness for you. You are saying I want to take responsibility for everything in my world and become aware of all things around me. You are saying that you want to practice a life of love, non-judgment, compassion and spirit.

Keep in mind the Universe of God does not jump into action effectively without a clear picture of what you want. When you are clear and declare who you are and what you want, the universe brings you the lessons which you need to understand to be what you want to be. This is how you raise your vibrations and create the world you want.

I remember when I was a child, I would ask God to bring me whatever I desired. What I realized is, if I did not declare who I was in this picture or dream then what I was asking God to bring me was only ever going to be a dream. An example: if I were to say I wanted to be a movie star and was not ready for the lessons needed to be a movie star then I would push everything away I was supposed to learn to get to that movie star vibration. When I said I wanted to start teaching and inspiring people, the universe started dropping books in my lap. The universe brought deep and meaningful spiritual guidance to living teachers, spiritual teachers, lessons to make me be stronger and many other things it would take for me to teach others about life and spirit. Some of those lessons included almost falling flat on my face! This led me to learn that I needed to be clear about what I wanted. I needed to declare I am a Child of God and therefore a part of a whole family. My declaration is, "I AM THAT GOD!" So are you, because God is not what we think it is. God is everything and we are that! We are made in God's image of pure love and by continuing to say this, I was less than perfect and only human. I was not giving credit to the fact I was made perfect just the way I am. When I did that, the world started unfolding for me. At first, I went at this with a sense of a large EGO saying that I AM GOD but not with love in my heart or humbleness, it was pure arrogance. What came from this arrogance is a series of people getting upset with me and thinking I *was* arrogant. This is because I was arrogant inside so arrogant people started to manifest around me. Then when my heart opened, I declared it again but this time it was with a light heartedness. When this happened, loving, humble and meek people started coming around me. Every step of the way, I had to learn how to let go of the people who were still stuck in their co-dependencies. I had to tell them the truth in order to stay in LOVE!

All of this has made me realize how remarkable life is and how blessed we truly are. So sit right now and declare who you are and know who you are!

This does not mean we do not work in the flow of the universe. The arrogance kept me from being in the flow because it blocked the flow. This is what it means when we are serving God because we are serving the higher goodness of us. The SOURCE creates all things. Declaring who we are is realizing our potential when we let go of all of our expectations and all our bonds of this limited planet so we can become cosmic. People twist this is with their EGO as I did with my EGO. In that sense, we get ourselves into trouble because we go into resistance of the love of God.

> *In the world of ideas it is the emotionally insecure who censure others while remaining prisoners of constricting ideologies and mindsets. Unable to handle too much knowledge, they find comfort in these narrow confines. It remains to the adventurous and unguarded that broad vistas open.*
> *Norman W. Turner*

Chapter 20
Discernment or Judgment?

People judged me for a great many things most of my life. I realized at an early age, people clouded the world with their judgment of how things should be done or should not be done and how we should look, act, or be. I have already covered a great deal of this topic throughout this book. I just wanted to touch on the difference between discernment and judgment because it was a hard concept for *me* to grasp.

In 2008, I asked in meditation; for God to teach me how not to judge. We need to really think about what we ask God and not take it lightly. My eyes opened to many people who pointed their fingers at me in judgment, gossiped about me, etc. Talk about asking and receiving, I received this lesson, not just tenfold but one hundred-fold! It was like sitting in my world and seeing all of my friends and loved ones pointing their fingers at me with shameful eyes. It was definitely an awakening experience but it was not because I thought they were bad people for pointing their finger in judgment, it was because I realized that I created this environment in my life. It was time to dive deep in this lesson to discover and become self-aware.

First, I had to look deep within myself and look at how *I* was judging *myself*. When I realized all the fingers pointed at me were just reflections of the fingers I pointed inside myself, I knew I could change. It was an incredible thought! I could change that self-judging voice in my head by just looking at how others were judging me. I thank them for being the messenger.

As I worked through this transition, I had a few close friends with whom I could process and talk about what was going on in my life. I described what was going on and how I felt but more importantly, how I changed this within myself and did not blame others for what I thought they did to me. While we discussed each other's life situations, it felt like we were judging the people we were processing about. I felt like a hypocrite. I felt we judged others and did not really work on ourselves. I realized I had to take ownership of my own feelings and only talk about situations happening now. I should not blame or talk badly about anyone else. By doing this I do not judge them, I process the situation to help heal my own inner demons.

I further processed the idea of judgment and discernment. I realized that discernment was a process of looking at what is the best path and what is not the best path. Discernment is a process of learning how to get more in tune with our soul's voice. The more we listen to that voice, the more we can experience the richness of life from our soul's perspective.

I realized discernment was a path for me to process my life and process the directions I wanted to go in life. It was also a process to get a richer relationship with myself. Judging is a process of pointing fingers and making someone responsible for what we do not want to look at in our own lives. Not looking at our own lives becomes an addiction. A classic example of this is a person who is upset their life is not going the way they want, so they blame others for their problems. They blame their boss for their job being miserable. They blame their spouse for having a hard life. These people are projecting their own insecure feelings onto others and not taking the opportunity to look at the mirror's reflection.

These reflections are golden treasures for us to look at, reflect on and help us grow even deeper as spiritual beings.

> *We cannot solve problems by using the same kind of thinking we used when we created them.*
> Albert Einstein

Chapter 21
Bringing It All Together

If I sat and pondered all I have learned throughout my life, and put it all together, it would have one consistent message, "Life is a constant practice, we can never learn too little and we are always learning and growing. When we think we have learned all that we need to learn, then we forfeit our rights to continue to live. Learning and growing are the very essences of life and the very essences of spirit."

Every experience in my life has made me a better person and has made me stronger in myself. As I got stronger in myself through my soul, I began to stand taller, be happier and find love all around me because I found a love for my experiences. I no longer resist the experiences I have. I embrace them because I know they help me grow as a spiritual being.

Throughout this book, I have consistently talked about self-awareness, listening to your inner voice, developing a better relationship with yourself and understanding yourself on a soulful level. Some ask me why I preach and talk about this consistent message more than other things. There is no other message we need to worry about. When we understand ourselves from a soulful level, everything falls into place. Our relationships get better, our relationship with God gets better and our intuitive abilities get better. We gain more love, more abundance in our lives and we gain a greater sense about life because our attitude about how we see things has shifted.

Since I have seen life through these eyes, my perspective has changed about many things. It does not mean I do not fall down, fall into my EGO, or do things against myself, I just use those opportunities to grow even stronger. The greatest gift we can give ourselves is our SELF.

Goodness comes from being good to yourself. When you can find that softness with yourself and a sense of knowing about yourself then you have arrived at a new level of love for yourself. This is the practice and this is how we create a life of peace within ourselves and within our world. Not only will we create peace because all things connect to us, but also because we will become the model to others. The more judgment and feelings of separation we can end within ourselves, the more this will change the world around us.

I watched this principle work countless times. Just know your thoughts are so powerful your anger can shake a ripple into the cosmos so massive it will effect everything. That kind of anger hurts you from the inside physically. It also effects the whole of God. Love is the highest vibration and the most powerful force in the universe. It is what creates everything around us. Love is GOD in its wholeness. Love is a flow, it is fluid not resistant but flows through the natural order of things.

My greatest advice to you is this: ***Do not get hung up in the words of men but allow your spirit to sing through you.*** Often times, we get hung up on words and are unable to enjoy the meaning of the message behind the words. This is the reason why the bible and many other books and texts like it; are twisted and used to hurt others. People take them literally and never through the heart. We try to make sense of it logically, instead of reading it with an open heart through love.

I have friends who do not understand why I use a lot of Christian texts in my writing or why I use them when I speak. It is because it rings true to me. Those people feel I am not teaching everything and that I am not including other religions in my teachings. I think all religions are limited but I think all texts show possibility. All texts have truths to them but when they are seen through the eyes of man (our human eyes) and not through the spirit of our Soul (our heart), these words are separated from the heart and we are not able to feel the message behind the words. This is how organizations of religion start, based on ideals of man and not through the spirit. These texts are meant to ignite the spirit within and allow your spirit to grow and manifest itself back into the glory that it is but organized religions fail because they do not teach their followers to interpret the messages with their soul.

It is time to declare the greatness that is you!

> *It is not necessarily the amount of time you spend at practice that counts; it is what you put into the practice.*
> *Eric Lindros*

Exercises

I wanted to give you a few exercises I have used throughout the years and found very effective in helping me in my journey. Remember, the idea here is to get to know yourself better, to get deeper into yourself and to find that deep love for yourself.

Remember, everything is a gradual process. If you are very depressed, you are not going to jump from depressed to happy overnight. It took me over a year of diligent practice to get to a deep meditation where I could feel the relaxing effects. Just be diligent in your quest to find yourself.

I also recommend writing your journey down so you can go back and look at who you were before. The purpose of journaling is not to live in the past; it is so you can fully appreciate your present. Some would say they could not think of anything to journal about. My suggestion is to start writing and allow whatever is in your mind to flow out of you. It could be "I woke up today to drink coffee and cannot believe I am writing in this silly journal." You get to work on your first judgment of yourself because "silly journal" is coming from a judgment that is blocking you. There is a mind chatter going on in you saying "Why are you doing something so silly?" You know you are just fine the way you are. Stop wasting your time. This is mind chatter!

In the end, I want you to make the decisions for yourself. You and your soul will decide the best path for you; I am merely telling you *my* truth. Find *your* own truth if mine does not fully resonate with *yours*. I know who I am, doing your own thing will not offend me at all and if it did, it would be about my insecurities, not yours. With that said, let us turn to the next page to see the first exercise.

The most important part of these meditations is to allow your imagination to flow and pay attention to the judgments, or mind chatter, going on in your mind. This allows you to look at all the things holding you back from bringing your mind into a quiet still place.

Mirror Work

For this exercise, you will need a mirror so you can stare directly into your eyes. The purpose of this is to spend time with yourself and look at yourself, allowing your mind to have anything that comes up to surface. Do not hold back on anything because many things might surface in your mind as you do this exercise. It could be your mind telling you how fat you are or how skinny you are. These are the opportunities for you. We all know you are a child of God and those judgments block you from seeing yourself truly in the light that you really are. You can use any type of mirror but my suggestion is to use one where you can see a good majority of your body.

Eye Work

This works very similar to Mirror Work except in this case you stand eye to eye with another person. The same principle . . . look at your mind chatter that comes up while you are looking into that person's eyes. Just like mirror work, you are connecting to your soul and you are connecting to their soul as well. On a much deeper level, you are connecting to the higher aspects of what is both of you. You are looking beyond the personalities to get to the core of who you both are. I highly recommend that couples do this on a regular basis.

Candle Flame

This exercise is to help focus your mind and to quiet the mind chatter. Take a pillar candle, light it, and put it on a table in front of you. Make the room completely dark and just stare into the flame. When you have a thought, whether it is good or bad, visualize throwing that thought into the flame. Eventually, after practicing this, your eyes will become off focus with the flame and you will be in a trance state with the flame. Having the intention to have a clear mind by throwing the thoughts in the flame your mind will eventually become very "STILL".

Connecting, Grounding, and Balancing

This exercise I learned from Virginia Drake. Stand up and take a deep breath in through your nose and then exhale through your nose. As you relax your body, I want you to visualize a small version of you dropping down into your heart. Pretend there is a little swing in your heart, so your smaller version of you can sit and swing back and forth in your heart. Then say with your inside voice "*Connect*." As you do this, visualize and feel golden energy coming down from the heaven; pouring from the top of your head down into your heart. Next, say with your inside voice "*Ground*." When you say this, visualize and feel green energy from the earth pouring up from your feet, up through your legs and connecting in your heart with the Golden Energy. Lastly say "*Balance*." When you do this, you allow the energy to balance from both the earth and the heavens. By doing this you honor both your human manifestation and God. Joining both energies, take a deep breath in through your nose and when you exhale out, I want you to push out. Allow the energy to push out and cover the cosmos as far as your imagination can take that energy. When you get as far as you can, pull it all back in, then push it back out again. Keep doing this...expand and contract that energy back and forth. This allows you to build yourself and make you stronger in who you are on an energetic level.

Prayer

Prayer to me is walking and talking with our soul, talking to that higher aspect of us and getting back into alignment with God. This is about developing that deep loving relationship with something greater than our physical manifestation. Start with meditation so you can go into your prayer with an open heart, ready to allow yourself to receive the wisdom or blessings you are asking from the divine. When you are open, you are ready to receive as much as you are ready to give. You will also find it very important to pray and bless food before you eat it as well as bless everything else going on around you. This keeps your mind in the state of knowing the world is full of blessings and you are appreciating everything in every moment.

Self-Energy Healing

This exercise is used as an enhancement to "Connecting, Grounding and Balancing." After you have achieved the state of being connected, grounded and balanced and you have practiced expanding and contracting yourself as far as your mind can stretch, take some time to just be still and allow yourself to feel anxieties, pains or muscle tension within your body. It is very important to breathe in through your nose and exhale out through your noise. As you do this, imagine passing the air you exhale in and out of your body so you can feel the tension, anxiety or any pain you have within your body. Those areas are areas to look within yourself and ask what your lesson is. I again pretend I am a smaller version of myself and sit there in that area of opportunity and just feel the tension or feel the pain. Say to this area "I am sorry I neglected you and did not give you the attention you needed. What lesson do I need to understand in order to release the pain and come back in to alignment?" Since you are already very open from connecting, grounding, and balancing, allow the energy to flow and open that area to help become aware and heal.

Loving Thyself / Mirror Work

Stand in front of a mirror, look straight into your eyes and say "I love you." Do this repeatedly and the important part of this exercise is to pay close attention to how your body is reacting to the love you are giving it. Does your body or face twitch? Do you have a feeling of anxiety when you say this? This is key because what is happening, is that your body is rejecting this love. It does not believe you. This is an area of opportunity for you. Ask your body "Where is my lesson? Where have I missed the mark of giving me the love I deserve?" This will give you areas to start processing how deep the self-talk goes within you.

About the Author

Accomplished spiritual healer and teacher, Jeremy E. McDonald has been a public speaker for over 14 years, and has designed and delivered many workshops to assist individuals helping them find peace and joy in their lives. Looking from an inside soul perspective, they are able to overcome fears, alchemizing them into love.

His clients find balance, peace, joy and true sublime self-love. For accolades of the world, Jeremy is a Reiki Master, EFT Practitioner, Theta healing practitioner, and Life Coach. He has served as a Key Note Speaker for everything from Expos, Colleges, and Professional Conferences to a small Workshop in a living room.

Jeremy is the host of the online radio show, Soul Talk, on V109fm.com, which discusses the transitory experience of knowing one's soul from an inner perspective. Guests include Spiritual Practitioners, Scientists, Medical Doctors, Musicians, and Artists having conversations of the Soul, coming together to enjoy the rewards of a soul driven by spirit, and guided by awareness of the self.

Peace

be still

*A path to self-awareness, love,
abundance, and harmony*

Jeremy E. McDonald